GRIEVING

The Pain
and the Promise

D0955123

DEANNA EDWARDS

Covenant Communications, Inc.

To my great-grandfather, Orson Pratt, who crossed a continent and helped to build a fortress. His last words were: "My body sleeps for a moment but my testimony lives and shall endure forever."

About the Author

Deanna Edwards is a composer, author, and singer whose songs bring peace to the sick, the elderly, and those who are grieving. She has written 200 songs and recorded 100 of them on ten albums. She conducts workshops throughout the United States and Canada, with recent tours in New Zealand and South Africa. She is the author of the book *Music Brings My Heart Back Home,* and she contributed to the book *Nursing Care of Children and Families: A Wholistic Approach.* She served for three years on the Foundation Board of Directors for the American College of Health Care Administrators. Her appearance on Voice for the Hurting with Sacred Heart Radio in St. Louis, Missouri, won the prestigious New York Radio Festival Award and the Religion in Media's Angel Award. She was selected by *Ladies' Home Journal* as one of the fifty American Heroines in 1984. She sings in sixteen languages and uses music in therapeutic settings as well as in teaching. Her song, "Teach Me to Die," was used on the NBC News Special "On Death and Dying." Her songs have also been used in films by the *American Journal of Nursing.* Deanna Edwards is an adjunct faculty lecturer in the Music Therapy Department at Utah State University. Deanna's husband, Cliff, is a professor at Brigham Young University. They are the parents of four sons.

Table of Contents

Acknowledgments

I wish to express my deep appreciation to all whose love and light have been of incalculable support in writing this book. Specifically, thanks to:

Cliff, wherever you go things grow. Your love has been fresh air and sunlight in my life.

To my sons: Shon, Steve, Jeff, and Eric. Your energy comes to me from wherever you are—Taiwan, Ecuador, England, or home. We are still one.

To Darla Hanks Isackson and my friends at Covenant Communications. The mission cannot be fulfilled until it is recognized. Your faith and your vision have sustained me.

To Bonnie Bright. You lightened my load and brightened my days. Our prayer in that little farmhouse was heard. He is still the wind beneath your wings.

To Ronnie. I got your message!

To Elder Todd Wilson and Elder Jeff Ball. Your testimonies live and shall endure forever.

To Shauna. Joseph Larsen walks in the presence of God, but he is still with us.

To the Donut Brigade: Pam, Barbara, Ann, Jerrolyn, Karen. You bring the world joy just by being yourselves! Keep on being!

To Roy Nichols and Dick Obershaw. You are a gift to those who grieve just as you have been to me. Thanks for letting me share you.

To Bears and Suzi Kaufman. After the rain came a rainbow from you.

To Dr. Tom Meyers. Your power to heal on the outside comes from the inside. The light is within you.

To Martin Gray. Your fortress shines in my heart.

To all my friends in Lincoln, Nebraska (you know who you are). Walk in the world for me.

To Dan and Irene Sperry for showing me the promise of spring hidden beneath the winter snows of adversity.

To Roger and Maria Swan. Thank you for letting me walk with you in darkness as well as the light.

To Roger Chapman. I will always hear you in the birds singing outside my window. You are greatly missed.

To Rosie. You have a great gift. Keep using it to help others.

To the Critchfield family, whose son, Stanley, lives not only in our hearts but in the hearts of the people of Ireland.

To my beloved sister, Miriam, whose death has taught me a new dimension of living and loving.

To my mother. When you went home you were not alone. God was holding your hand.

To Father Rick. We celebrate with you your new birthday! In dying, you were born into eternal life!

And, finally, to the countless friends without whose contributions and insights this book could not have been written. Your gracious permission to share your poems and letters and ideas are deeply appreciated. You are my heroes.

Preface

This book, *Grieving: The Pain and the Promise*, has been a work of love, and represents the combined efforts of many courageous people. So often when we speak of pain it is in hushed reference to the possibilities of enduring it, surviving it, coping with it, tolerating it, or seeking ways to avoid it.

This book is about learning to live *with* grief as companion and teacher. It is about looking into the face of pain and acknowledging the fact that joy and pain are companions, each inseparable from the other.

We cannot see the promise without accepting the consequences of pain. The promise of new life, new insight, new growth, and a new awareness of our Savior's divine mission could not be ours if we turned our eyes away from the pain that made it all possible.

So, I express my thanks to those who have shared with me a sacred trust, for each person's grief is sacred. I will hold your pain gently in my heart and celebrate with you the glorious promise of greater joy to come. All is well!

Deanna Edwards

CHAPTER ONE

What Is Grief?

It was a soft, summer evening filled with the sound of crickets. A gentle breeze whispered the scent of corn and clover through an open window as my husband and I sat reading the newspaper. Our three little boys had been tucked into bed and were sound asleep when suddenly the quiet peace of the night was shattered by an explosion. There had been an automobile collision nearby. I rushed to the telephone, dialed 911, and asked for emergency help. With the terrible impact still ringing in our ears, Cliff and I climbed on our bicycles, hoping to be of help at the scene of the accident. We had only been riding for a short time when, to our horror, we saw that our bicycles were heading directly for some power lines that had just been knocked down by the impact of a car. It was too late for us to stop or turn around. We were upon the lines and in danger of becoming entangled in them. Death was only inches away, and I knew it. I remembered a handsome athlete who had been killed by power lines in my hometown of Logan because he had stopped to render assistance at an accident site. Amazingly, the first impression that came into my mind was not one of fear. It was the awareness that I was totally unprepared for death. I was prepared to live, not to die! In my mind, I could see the shelves of fruits and vegetables and the storage cans full of wheat and rice in our food supply.

We had no guardian for the children. There was no will. We had never talked about death in family home evening. The children, who were peacefully sleeping, could awaken to learn that their parents had been killed instantly. I said a fervent prayer: "Heavenly Father, we are not prepared for this moment. Please make a miracle, Father, and give us more time!"

Miraculously, we crossed the power lines safely. A fireman who had just arrived on the scene looked at us incredulously. "I think the rubber tires on your bicycles saved your lives!" he exclaimed.

Convinced that help had come from a higher source, we returned home, shaken but determined to prepare our children and teach them about an important subject that we had never dared to mention. It was not difficult to talk about birth, about what color to paint their nurseries, or what name we would choose to give them. But death and grief were not subjects we had been prepared to deal with. We wanted to define for our children and for ourselves what grief is and the process we would go through if we were faced with catastrophic loss.

The next day we explained to them the dangers we had encountered the night before. We told them it was possible that both Mom and Dad could die at the same time, and how death was as much a part of Heavenly Father's plan as birth. We explained that if something were to happen that resulted in our deaths, they would have to go and live with another family who would lovingly raise them. We asked them to think about all their aunts, uncles, and cousins and tell us who they would be most comfortable living with. We also phoned for an appointment with a lawyer so we could select a guardian for the children and get our will in order. We have since had occasional family home evenings in which we have discussed the meaning of death and outlined the many challenges and special needs of those who grieve.

Grief is our emotional, physical, spiritual, and intellectual response to loss. It is the overwhelming involvement of all of our senses to deprivation. In its many forms, grief comes to all. It can strike us in unexpected ways at any moment in our lives. It reminds us how vulnerable we are and how fragile life is. Grief is inseparably connected to our capacity to love. The depth of our grief is in direct proportion to the clarity and care with which we have loved.

When we grieve, we may believe no one could have felt the same pain and that no one will feel it as deeply after us. In a way, that is true, for our feelings of love and grief are unique to us and entirely personal. Yet it is the uniqueness of our capacity to feel love and sorrow that binds us to all humankind. Because we are children of God, we are his only creations to experience such intensity of emotion when death separates us. It is our universal capacity to love which provides the awareness that grief transcends all barriers of race and religious denominations. A common thread among all the contributions from grieving people included in this book is the belief that death is not the end of loving relationships. There is universal hope for continuation, for eternal ties. Like the tiny snowflake that melts but is not extinguished forever, these relationships change only in form. But changes can be painful, and the natural and universal response to change is grief.

The expression of grief is not the evidence of a lack of faith. It is simply the evidence of our love and our need to find closure as we examine new ways to continue our lives in different directions. The practical aspect of grief is that life must go on, and we must have the courage to redefine our place in the shifting landscape of our existence. Death is something we should learn about and prepare for just as we prepare ourselves and our loved ones to live and to survive during our experiences in mortality.

Laurene Cunningham wrote: "When the tragedy of death visits, there is no gift of manual dexterity, no intellectual scheme, no credit card with enough clout, no human device imaginable that can protect us. We are stripped of all our 'grown-up' buffers and reminded, in a startling way, just how little control we have in life's plan. I believe that whether you are six or seventy-six, when a loved one dies, you feel somewhat abandoned."[1]

So often when we think about grief, we focus only on the physical death of someone we love, forgetting the other deep, deathlike wounds that touch people's lives every day. What does it feel like to experience a divorce or to lose the love and respect of a cherished friend who finds forgiveness a difficult gift to give? What does it mean suddenly to lose physical capabilities through accident or catastrophic illness? What of parents who, in spite of dedicated teaching, have experienced the loss of a child who trips and falls into temptation and rebellion? How do people feel when they have been the victims of sexual, physical, or emotional abuse? How do couples feel when they are told they can never have a child of their own to love and nurture? What of those families who must live daily with the struggles of caring for a severely handicapped child or with the mental illness of a loved one? How do these people feel when they are silently ostracized by those who are afraid their grief will be contagious? How do they feel when their needs are not addressed by a society which denies the realities of death, old age, and pain?

Roy Nichols, a funeral director and grief counselor from Chagrin Falls, Ohio, wrote: "In an American society which is so defiant about death; which reveres youth so highly; which conceals the aged and the ill in institutions; which portrays death in the media as tragic, horrible, unlawful, unwanted, seldom as peaceful; which wants everything so comfortable and so convenient; which attempts to manipulate and control its environment; in that kind of society death is frequently interpreted as an insult, as an intruder, as unnecessary, as superimposed on life; the acceptance of death and the

---

[1] Letter to author, West Springfield, Massachusetts. Used by permission.

resulting ability to move through grief work is severely inhibited by the notion that death and pain cannot possibly be a part of the American Dream and the Good Life."[2]

Spencer W. Kimball said, "Being human, we would expel from our lives physical pain and mental anguish and assure ourselves of continual ease and comfort, but if we were to close the doors upon sorrow and distress, we might be excluding our greatest friends and benefactors. Suffering can make saints of people as they learn patience, long-suffering, and self-mastery."[3]

The concept of grief as a friend and benefactor was intriguing to me and caused me to reflect on the gift of grief and the promise of it as I wrote these lines:

Death, who?

I pretend I do not know you
Yet you are always by my side,
Warning me to tell the children
Not to run into the street
Or go too close to the edge of the river,
Urging me to drive carefully.
You govern my life, yet you have no name
For I have not given you one.
But when I meet you face-to-face
You are not always so terrifying
For you make me aware
Of how much I can love.

Spencer W. Kimball often quoted an anonymous poem that speaks of pain as mentor and teacher:

Pain stayed so long I said to him today, "Be gone!
I will not have you with me any more!"
I paused there, startled at the look he wore.
"I who have been your friend," he said to me,

---

2 Nichols, Roy and Jane, "Funerals: A Time for Grief and Growth" in Elisabeth Kubler-Ross, *Death, the Final Stage of Growth.*
3 Kimball, Spencer W., *Tragedy or Destiny?* (Salt Lake City, Utah: Deseret Book, 1977), p. 3.

"I who have been your teacher—all that you know
Of understanding love, of sympathy,
And patience, I have taught you. Shall I go?"
He spoke the truth, this strange unwelcome guest;
I watched him leave and knew that he was wise.
He left a heart grown tender in my breast.
He left a far, clear vision in my eyes.
I dried my tears, and lifted up a song
Even for one who'd tortured me so long."[4]

Ted Lofgreen shared the following special thought that brought a smile to my heart. "In a church meeting an instructor posed the question, 'Of all the problems in life, which would be the hardest to face?' After several people gave their answers, one said, 'Death. I think death would be my hardest trial.' His instructor replied, 'That's what I used to think, but you know, thanks to the Lord, death is like all our other problems. We'll live through it.'"

When we are living in the season of grief we have no choice. We have to go through it, but with the promise that we will also live through it in the eternal sense. The question then becomes, "How do I live through this?" Neal A. Maxwell wrote, "Rather than simply passing through trials, we must allow trials to pass through us in ways that sanctify us. Thereby, our empathy, too, is enriched and everlasting."[5] Grief expands our souls with the awareness of how much we have loved, but that expansion can extract a painful price. How do we live through the present moments and the day-to-day struggles with pain, the companion, walking constantly at our side? A song I wrote, "That's Enough," carries a significant message in one of the verses. "I had to learn so many things and fail so many times before the day I finally realized if we could take the sorrow from every loss that comes along, we'd have to take the loving out of life."

---

[4] *Ibid.* p. 5.
[5] Maxwell, Neal A., "Enduring Well," *Ensign,* April 1997.

One evening as I was preparing for bed and listening to the evening news I heard that a young missionary, Elder Stanley Critchfield, had been stabbed to death by an assailant as he and his companion were entering their apartment in Ireland. I quickly dressed, called the family, and asked if I could assist them in any way. They said they would appreciate a visit. His casket was being flown home the following day and they were anticipating not getting much sleep. I asked my son to join me, and as we were driving toward the little town of Payson in the darkness I said, "Shon, do you feel as much at a loss for words as I do?" He nodded, and I said, "On our way back to Provo tonight we will feel differently."

We were warmed and welcomed by Carol and Gayle Critchfield who hugged us and invited us in to the warm farmhouse. "We are so glad you came!" Carol said. Immediately they showed me pictures and scrapbooks of a handsome and accomplished young man. We were introduced to grandparents, golden haired sisters and a younger brother. As we gathered in the kitchen I sang the song, "That's Enough," and asked if anyone in the room would be willing to forfeit their capacity to love so they would never have to hurt again. Each one in the room said "No!" The love and joy they had experienced with Stanley could never be traded away for indifference. Over the coming months we became good friends, and we were able to meet some of the people who had come from Ireland who had known and loved Stanley. A few years later, Carol called and asked me if I could sing at a farewell for their younger son, who had also been called to the Doublin, Ireland mission. He continued his brother's work and arrived home safely.

If we could be promised we would never experience the terrible pain of loss but would have to relinquish our capacity for love in the process, who would make that trade? Perhaps the first step in learning to live with grief is the awareness that love is, indeed, worth the price we have to pay for it.

In previous years, I had known only the comfortable world of home and family. I was not closely involved with the sick, the dying, and the grieving until my Relief Society president, Shirley Hoffman, invited me to become a volunteer with her at Mennonite Hospital in Bloomington, Illinois. The decision to become a volunteer changed my life and compelled me to look more closely at the face of death. I had to come to grips with my own fears and feelings about death, aging, and illness in order to more effectively help the patients and residents I served. Once I was able to overcome my own fears and my denial of my father's death, I found that I had much to learn about life and living from those who were dying. A nurse who worked with me in the hospital loved music as I did, and we began a music program, singing to patients throughout the hospital, including those in the intensive care unit. The more I listened to the needs and feelings expressed by the patients, the more I realized their needs had not been addressed in musical literature. They lived in a musical void because their feelings were not "commercial." The only songs heard on the radio were songs about "commercial" feelings of falling in and out of love. There were no songs to reflect the experiences of patients who suffered with prolonged illness and pain. My first attempt to give my own father a musical voice resulted in a song for all those who were faced with life-threatening illnesses. I titled it, "Teach Me To Die."

Sunlight filters through my window falling from the sky.
Time slips like a silent stranger softly passing by.
Life goes on in busy circles leaving me behind.
Memories like portraits fill the attic of my mind.

I know that it isn't easy seeing me this way,
And it hurts to watch me lying here day after day.
Trade your fear of parting for the faith that knows no pain.
Don't be afraid to say "Good-bye"; I know we'll meet again!

Teach me to die. Hold onto my hand.
I have so many questions, things I don't understand.

Teach me to die. Give all you can give.
If you'll teach me of dying, I will teach you to live! 6

I had little hope that we would ever find a publisher for a song about death, but when NBC News did a television special, "On Death and Dying," featuring the pioneering work of Elisabeth Kubler-Ross, I was invited to sing the song. The program was sponsored by the United Catholic Conference. The production manager, Joan Paul, was visibly moved by the song, and she sent it to the Franciscan Communications Center in Los Angeles. They wrote to me, offering me a recording contract.

I felt it would be wise to seek spiritual counsel concerning the decision I had to make. Joseph R. Larsen was then president of the Champaign Illinois Stake, as well as a beloved friend. He was a man who had known great adversity in his own life and had always triumphed over it. In 1953 he had been driving alone on a Maryland highway when the steering mechanism on his jeep failed. He catapulted through the metal roof, landing about forty-five feet away. He suffered a broken neck and a badly damaged spinal cord. After fervent prayer, his life was spared, but he was told he would spend the rest of his life in a wheelchair. In spite of his paralysis, he lived a highly accomplished and dedicated life, becoming an inspiration to all who knew him. His latest assignment was director of the Division of Rehabilitation-Education Services at the University of Illinois at Champaign-Urbana. He was responsible for the physical and emotional well-being of all the disabled students on campus.

He quickly developed a keen interest in my work in music therapy and invited me to sing at many functions. He always requested his favorite song, "He Ain't Heavy; He's My Brother." I will never forget a special occasion when he asked

---

6 Edwards, Deanna. "Teach Me To Die," from the album *Peacebird*, Rock Canyon Music Publishers, 777 East Walnut Ave., Provo, Utah 84604.

me if I would accompany him to the hospital to sing for a beloved granddaughter who was ill. I arrived with him, my guitar in tow. Since he had undergone surgery himself only days before, I thought naively that I could carry my guitar with one arm and help to push his wheelchair with the other.

As we started down the long hallway, he suddenly disappeared before my very eyes. I was startled to see him zoom ahead in his wheelchair, and disappear around a corner. "Wait for me!" I exclaimed, as I struggled to catch up with him.

His eyes were twinkling. "I'll do the wheelchair," he smiled. "You do the singing. If you just sing you can have anything you want for dinner, including chocolate cake!"

When I told President Larsen that I had been offered a recording contract by a company in Los Angeles he said without hesitation, "Deanna, you have an important musical mission ahead of you. There are times when that mission will require great sacrifice from you and your family, but the Lord will assist you in this work and will help you to care for your family as well. This will be only one of many opportunities for you to render service to those who need you. I want the first album off the press!"

He became my greatest supporter and a constant source of strength. Whenever I would call him with a new project or to sing a song I had just written, he would say, "Ah, the petals are just beginning to unfold. There will be more to come."

Little did I realize then that one day I would be called upon to be a strength to him—to sing at his bedside as he fought agonizing battles with cancer. The deep, easy peace in his voice was always there. "The Lord is my physician," he used to say with the confidence of one who had known his Creator personally.

Neal A. Maxwell spoke at his funeral service February 24, 1989. He shared with us a message from the First Presidency of The Church of Jesus Christ of Latter-day Saints. Directed to Shauna Larsen and their family, it was a great source of comfort to us all.

Dear Sister Larsen,

It was with deep regret that we learned of the passing of your husband, Joseph R. Larsen, Jr., whom we loved and admired very much. We extend our love and condolences to you and to your family at this time of bereavement. At the same time, we rejoice with you in your husband's life and dedicated service, especially his faithfulness and courage in serving so well for ten years as president of the Champaign Illinois Stake, in spite of the handicap that required his being in a wheelchair.

To those who have a testimony of the gospel of Jesus Christ, death is not a tragedy but is an essential step in the journey leading to exaltation. Joseph Larsen has merely gone ahead to continue his labors in another sphere and to prepare for the happy reunion which awaits you there. May the Lord be with you and yours to give you peace and comfort at this time of trial and to sustain and guide you in the years ahead.

Faithfully your brethren,
Ezra Taft Benson,
Gordon B. Hinckley,
Thomas S. Monson[7]

That there is pain in grief as well as the potential for growth and peace is evident in the letter from the First Presidency. There is recognition of the earthly suffering experienced when a loved one dies, but also a reminder of the eternal joy that awaits us in the life to come.

If we focus only on death and the earthly pain that separation causes us, the comfort and promise of eternal life is obscured from our vision. On the other hand, if we focus attention only on the promise of seeing our loved ones again someday and the blessings of eternal life, the pain inherent in mortal experience can go unrecognized and the very real needs of those who grieve are not addressed. The pain and

---

[7] From Shauna Larsen. Used by permission.

the promise must be recognized together so that we can meet the needs of both the mortal and spiritual condition.

When Ed J. Pinegar was president of the London South Mission, his seventeen-year-old son was killed in Utah in an automobile accident. My own sons had known Cory and the great contributions of his short life. I asked President Pinegar about his impressions of that experience, and he said, "When Cory died, I grew more in one year than I did in my fifty previous years because I submitted my will to God. Our strength is in the Lord, and our submission to His will brings joy and peace. When I think of my son in the mortal sense, I miss him so deeply. When I think of him spiritually I know that he is doing his work as I am doing my work. As birth is to mortality, so likewise is death to immortality and eternal life."

Dr. Martin Israel said, "One in pain is removed from the surface of the world and has to withdraw into his own being. The theme of spiritual growth is one of withdrawal followed by return. But the person who returns after the harrowing withdrawal that follows suffering is changed, and in turn brings that change to the world around him."

We can be privileged to become the students of those who have "returned following the harrowing withdrawal of suffering." I have met these great teachers as I have looked into the faces of the old, into the youthful faces of dying children, and into the eyes of those who have met immense suffering with grace and equanimity. I have seen it in the expressions of honest pain in letters that come to me daily from people who have the courage to share.

Those who grieve are well qualified to become our teachers. They have stood at the very threshold of life, and they understand the true meaning of love. They have a vision and awareness that far surpasses those whose lives have never been pierced with deep pain and suffering. They speak to us honestly and courageously from the heart of the refiner's fire. They understand the importance of values and priorities. They are deeply sensitive. They will no longer trust in superficial answers or well-worn clichés. They guard against those who are afraid of their pain and too uncomfortable to communicate in an authentic way. They are impatient with those who have learned to use their faith in life after death as a reason to avoid doing the work of grief, or those who believe grief is unnecessary in the presence of faith. They do not care how much we know until they know how much we care. Once they discover that we are unafraid, that we are willing to learn from them and that we are nonjudgmental, they will tell us what it is like to walk with pain as a companion. Though they may never receive a diploma from the school of suffering, they, both young and old, will teach us to live and love as we never have before. They will render themselves vulnerable for our sakes, and if we learn the lessons they have to teach us, our lives will never be the same again.

Roy Nichols said, "The most beautiful people we have known are those who have known defeat, known suffering, known struggle, known loss, and have found their way out of the depths. These persons have an appreciation, a sensitivity, and an understanding of life that fills them with compassion, gentleness, and a deep loving concern. Beautiful people do not just 'happen.' Growth can come in unexpected ways from the nooks and crannies of our life's experiences. In death and in grief we do not need so much protection from painful experiences as we need the boldness to face them. We do not need as much to be tranquilized from pain as we need the strength to conquer it. If we choose to love, we must also have the courage to grieve. What a blessing to take time to pause from our well-meant efficiency and to realize that when a love is lost, our capacity to love is not lost also. From our grief can come growth."[8]

---

[8] *Ibid.*

Those who have dared to share their innermost thoughts and feelings concerning their own pain in the following pages have demonstrated great courage. I deeply respect the heroic efforts of people to pick up their shattered dreams and find greater meaning and purpose in their suffering. Their insight will be a light to us when we are called to look upon the face of pain.

CHAPTER TWO

What Is Grief Work?

"In the truest, deepest sense, grief work is love work." I made the statement at a women's conference and was greeted afterward by a sandy-haired young woman with tear-filled eyes. She told me of the long struggles involved in going on with her life without her mother and the effects of her mother's lengthy illness and death on her life.

"I've wondered why I had to carry such pain all this time," she said. "Tonight you helped me to realize that I was not just holding my own pain. I was also holding my mother's love."

Grief is not a disease. It is the hardest work we will ever have to do. Grief counselors have long considered the activity associated with grief as "work." The awareness that grief is hard work was a wonderful revelation for me. I had previously considered grief to be debilitating and depressing, but I have learned that there is a big difference between depression and grief work. Depression can be caused by chemical imbalance, mental illness or physical illness. For many of us, however, depression is a prolonged state of self-concern that is destructive to us and to the people we love. It is a way of focusing only on our own needs and our own worries. On the other hand, grief work requires physical, spiritual, emotional and intellectual determination. *It is the labor involved in dissolving physical bonds, while allowing our spiritual bonds to remain intact.* When pain, loneliness, emptiness, and separation cause us to lose control, grief work is the process necessary to take control back into our lives. The natural response to loss is a feeling of grief. Work is the action we take that concerns the process of regaining control of our *response* to what happens to us. Growth is the aftermath of grief work. We must *go* through to *get* through.

What we resist, persists. Our determination to avoid doing grief work does not make the work go away. If your house needs to be cleaned you can spend days avoiding the process of entering your home and doing the necessary cleaning. But avoidance will not make the work go away. And so it is with grief. Avoiding the work of grief will not make it disappear. I call it, "Going the distance." Just as an athlete struggles to complete a race, a parent goes the distance with a child, from birth, until death separates them. We might also call it "enduring to the end."

When his own father died, funeral director Roy Nichols from Chagrin Falls, Ohio, stumbled across an important clue in grief work: *personal involvement.* As strangers prepared to take care of his father, he found he wanted to be involved. He plunged into the grief work headlong: took care of the death certificate, notified the newspapers, arranged for and planned the funeral service, and handled all the details accompanying the task of being a funeral director.

He was functioning in a dual role, as a funeral director and as a son. He said, "I didn't need to be a funeral director. I needed to be a son, and I wanted to attend to the details myself. It was my dad, it was my job, and it was our love."

His entire family became a part of the experience, sharing responsibilities and renewing childhood closeness. They carried their father to the grave and buried him with their own hands. They closed out his life together.

It wasn't until weeks later that it dawned on him what had happened. He was able to participate actively in the experience of his father's death and the grief work was begun immediately. He began to wonder how many others had felt lost because he, as a funeral director, had done everything for them. How many people had been delayed in their grief work because he, as the functionary, had usurped their role as care-giving family members, making decisions without consulting them, because he assumed they "couldn't handle it." Immediately, his role in funeral service shifted to that of *facilitating.*

Roy has written one of the finest articles I have read concerning grief work and has given me permission to share it with you. It is comprehensive but contains concepts that we can relate to when faced with our own experiences with grief. In this article he has also included valuable suggestions from Tom Attig, Ph.D., Department of Philosophy, Bowling Green State University.

On May 17, 1982, Jim died unexpectedly in a single car accident. The cause of the accident remains unknown. I met with his family in their home and was impressed in several ways. This was a particularly warm, loving, closely knit family unit of Mom, Dad, and eight other children, Jim being the oldest of the nine. There were articles in the home which had been made by various family members—pottery, macrame, and wall hangings. This was a talented family. It was also very evident that encouragement and permission to develop unique personalities was strong. These eight children were very much individual parts and also part of the whole. What resulted was an unusual funeral experience. When they arrived at my funeral home to finalize details, they had decided on an evening mass at their church because it would be more accessible to people. They wanted the public expression of love, support and community. When I showed them caskets, they were visibly uncomfortable. These weren't Jim. So we explored other options. I suggested a rough, sawed, cedar lumber box and drew a sketch. The next day two carpenters made a rectangular-shaped casket with rope loop handles. A neighbor brought in several bedding articles—a pillow, blanket, sheet, mattress, sleeping bag, etc. Jim's dad helped arrange the interior of the casket and he helped lift Jim into the casket. Natural materials from home were used to line the casket, and it was Jim because it represented his values, beliefs, and lifestyle.

There were about 400 people at the evening mass. Jim's brothers and sisters were the pallbearers. The family had very carefully planned the liturgy with the priest and participated in the mass. The brothers and sisters and parents placed the casket on the web straps and lowered it into the concrete box. They placed the lid on the box. Shovels were provided and, family first, then friends, filled in the grave. When the dirt had been mounded over the grave, several knelt in a circle and smoothed the dirt, tossing stones and clods into the woods. Dad opened a large box of grass seed and wandered through the people, pouring seed into cupped hands. We all gathered around the grave and sowed the seed over the fresh grave. One person sang a song that came to mind. Many lingered for a long time, trying to integrate and comprehend what had been experienced. More love than dirt had been put into the grave.

Later, at the family's home, I noticed a large display of pictures of Jim had been mounted on a board and placed on the fireplace mantel. More pictures were stacked nearby. They were beginning the painful conversion from presence to memory.

The funeral experience was not one of professionals, but one of family and friends. As the funeral director, my functional role was very minimal.

As care givers, we need to take care that we do not reinforce feelings of helplessness in those who are grieving. Helplessness produces three deficits. (1) It undermines the motivation to respond, to fight. (2) It retards the ability to learn that responding does work. (3) It results in emotional disturbance, primarily anxiety and depression. When a traumatic experience occurs or threatens to occur, it causes a heightened state of fear. Fear continues until one of two things happens. If the person learns that the trauma can be controlled, fear is reduced and may disappear altogether. If the person learns (or believes) that the trauma is beyond control, fear will be replaced with anxiety, depression, and helplessness. Life is experienced as being utterly uncontrollable. Control is the major issue. The cure (or therapy) is to find a way of exercising control.

The critical difference between those who recover well and those who never quite recover from trauma is in whether the attempt to control is limited to controlling one's own response to the traumatic experience or whether the attempt to control is extended to the traumatic experience itself. Let me explain.

We all experience death, disappointment, embarrassment, and losses of varying kinds. Some confront the loss by admitting it, telling about it, and sharing it. The focus of control is to acknowledge the loss, do the grief work and redefine one's role in relationship to life. Others limit the acknowledgement of that trauma by not telling about it, not admitting it, not sharing it, and not confronting it. A kind of denial, it is an attempt to control experiences of life by refusing to acknowledge them and by avoiding dealing with the experiences. In funeral-related behavior, this is expressed in private funerals, in closed caskets, in funerals where the body is not present, in not going to the grave following the funeral ritual, in using a cemetery chapel building for the committal rather than the site of the grave, etc. An extreme example of trying to control the traumatic experience is to simply make no public announcement that a death has occurred, have no funeral ritual of any kind, and not see the person dead. Thus, the focus of control is extended to controlling the total experience rather than the self in relationship to the experience. I believe people who approach the death of loved ones in this manner do not recover well.

Jim's family focused issues of control on the individuals, not on the experience itself. It was clear to me that the family was creative, a family of doers, who were involved and active. I could have engaged that family with an approach that conveyed, "This is so tragic. These things shouldn't have happened. This is more than you should have to bear. You can't possibly handle this. Let me take care of this for you." An air of despair and victimization would have been cast over the entire experience. They would have become passive, help-less bystanders to their life experience. They could have even been convinced that they were so immobilized that they couldn't even drive their own car. I'd send a car for them! When the approach to a family conveys the victimized, help-less message, the message is debilitating and the result is depression. With Jim's family, the approach would have forced them to abort their successful strategy for coping. Instead, they were permitted, even encouraged, to stay on their feet, to engage in the decision-making process, to fight, to grapple with the life experience, and to demonstrate that even when life is horrible, they can still function as a family, can still perform, be active, cope and live on.

The well-known fight/flight syndrome directly applies. When an animal senses danger or threat, the response is to fight or to flee. No animal simply remains idly by to allow what will be. So, too, with the human animal. Jim's family were persons whose coping strategy was not to flee when sensing danger or threat. They were fighters. If I as a funeral director had imposed the passive state of being, a critical error may have been made which would have had long-standing implications on the emotional well-being of the family and individual persons.

Forest was born on April 27, 1982. He was just two-and-a-half-months old. The father, not the nurse, phoned me from the hospital to report the baby's death. That told me some-thing. We talked for awhile. I followed a gut feeling and asked if he wanted me to go to the hospital and get his baby's body or whether he would be comfortable bringing the body to me. His response was immediate. He checked with his wife and she affirmed his response. It took awhile to convince the nurse that the baby's body was legally the property of the parents, not the nurse, me, the nurse's institution, or my institution. They had the legal right to walk out with their child and didn't even have to sign the release form. It was their baby. Institutional policy could not stop them.

They arrived with their baby, held him, talked to him. They built his coffin the next day. About forty people gathered for the funeral. These young parents conducted the ritual, explaining as best they could what death meant to them, according to their personal beliefs. Mostly they just admitted they didn't know but were struggling to learn. They did believe that death is not extinction. Their car was used for the hearse. At the grave the parents placed the coffin in the hole and several people passed dirt hand to hand until the grave was filled. A song was sung. A potted mum plant was placed in the soil.

The parents demonstrated to themselves that even when life is horrible, they could remain in control. *They could not control what life was doing to them, but they could control what they did with what life was doing to them.* They could maximize the experience to create an opportunity to learn about themselves, to explore a coping strategy, to learn to manage feelings by confronting and permitting those feelings. When you carry your dead baby from the hospital, make his coffin, explain to your family and friends what you believe about death, and bury him, feelings are released. It was the expression of those feelings that created the opportunity to learn how one can control the response of self to life experience. A person learns a new way of control and can circumvent unneeded fear, anxiety, depression, and helplessness. If the parents had shifted the focus of control from response of self to life experience to the life experience itself, they wouldn't have actively participated in any of the functions, and perhaps not participated at all.

The surrogate sufferer is one who would attempt to suffer in the place of the sufferer in the hope of reducing the suffering of the sufferer. A pervasive pattern in care giving among professionals and nonprofessionals alike, it encompasses all attempts to shield persons subject to care from painful or otherwise difficult experiences. An attempt to run interference on pain, it is truly a well-intentioned strategy for care giving; tragically, however, the intention is seldom realized. Perhaps never. Can one cry the tears for another? Do the grief work for another? Solve the problems for another? Jesus did not solve the problems for those to whom he ministered. He simply gave them the tools by which they could solve their own problems.

The surrogate suffering syndrome is rooted in feelings of helplessness. Both those in need and those trying to help are subject to such feelings. Both struggle with what to say and do. Both seek ways of functioning meaningfully in the face of tragedy. Both are groping for control. In struggling for a way of "helping," if our helping mode is "Let me do this for you," we mitigate our own sense of helplessness. We feel better having "helped." *Those needing help are left passive, uninvolved spectators to the drama of life, and their feelings of helplessness are not addressed.*

The alternative mode in care giving is to help sufferers to function for themselves. Such an approach mitigates the helplessness of both the sufferer and the care giver. The result is increased feelings of competence and satisfaction among care givers as they succeed in helping those in their care to function meaningfully.

It is necessary to stress that the surrogate suffering syndrome is not just typical of caring professionals; it is a dominant pattern in society as a whole. The surrogate suffering syndrome is merely a reflection of a deep-seated problem.

Critical reflection on our own behavior is especially difficult. It can hurt deeply to discover the very real possibility that good intentions can have the effect of making the suffering worse. How could my helping compound human suffering? The discovery can be especially difficult for the caring professional who has brought abundant good intentions and dedication to the caring process, and who has tried again and again to give the best of care to those who are hurting. One must, however, be willing to examine seriously, very carefully, and very deeply, issues of helplessness and of control, and to examine more sensitive responses to human suffering. The process is agonizing but rewarding.

Perhaps the surrogate suffering syndrome is a defense mechanism we adopt to spare ourselves the difficult task of dealing immediately and directly with the suffering of another. It is difficult to be present as another is suffering deeply. However, when we realize that the strategy of sparing suffering is likely to fail, it will provide us less satisfaction.

To be certain, the large majority of my funeral practice is very conventional and I do my "surrogate sufferer thing" because that is the norm and what is expected. Should I do otherwise, I would offend the expectation. Most are raised in families and settings where institutional policies encourage and reinforce the syndrome. The broader social context expects such behavior. *Most have learned that you hire professionals to manage your stress and to function in your place.* Many have been taught to flee and turn away in the fight/flight response to danger and threat. The challenge is to identify that person or family who would choose to employ a different strategy and would choose to solve their own problems.

One of the reasons we Americans are observing a trend in the minimization of funerals is because people have been having funerals but not really experiencing them due to their passive roles. Professionals, because they do the doing, are more likely to understand the value because they have had the active experience. Without question, Jim's family and Forest's family will have funerals in the future because they have had valuable experiences.

I had a marvelous lesson a few years ago with a Protestant minister and his social worker wife. Her elderly mother was living with them and died at home. I went to their home and performed necessary but minimal functions. Then I left. They cared for her body at home, did her hair, dressed her, left her in bed, and held the visitation in their home. Those who wanted to see Grandma did so in her bedroom. Two days later I drove to the home with the casket in my hearse. The family carried the casket indoors and placed Grandma in it. We went to church for the funeral.

Later I learned why they did what they did. Very early in their marriage they had a child die. It nearly destroyed their relationship, taking them over twenty years to recover from the death. They shared that they had merely disposed of the child's body without pausing to experience the death of their child. Having examined that experience, they decided they had erred and decided on a different attack the next time.

I would be very foolish if I were to claim that their prolonged suffering was because they did not have a funeral for their child. Funerals don't work miracles; they only begin to assuage human suffering. I will claim, however, that to repeat the second time a strategy that failed the first time would have been a mistake. Because I am acquainted with these people, I know that the second strategy was far more fulfilling and will probably be repeated.

Emotional suffering may be experienced fast and hard and painfully, or slowly and hard and painfully. There doesn't seem to be another way.

There is a well-grounded principle in creativity known as "deferred judgment." Very early I begin telling the family that they will have certain decisions to make along the way. I give them information in advance and give them time to consider their options. It is their life, their love, their grief, their memories, their experience, their mental health. They should structure that experience just the way they want it for themselves. I am simply with them in the experience.

Most of us adapt better to facts, data and real experience rather than to the void of these. One cannot experience too much reality so long as one is voluntarily experiencing reality and because the experience is a chosen one. One can, for certain, experience too little reality. When reality is not experienced, the reality is fabricated in the fantasy. Observe any kid. *The fantasized reality is usually, if not always, worse than the truth.* The concept of deferred judgment is probably the helping concept I use most in my funeral practice. It is simply advising that a question will be asked later. For example: "Tomorrow, when the minister is finished with his message, I will quietly ask you if you want to leave the room when I close the casket, or if you want to be here when I do that, or if you want to help me do it." Another: "When you bring in his clothes, please tell me if you want to put his wedding band on his finger or if I should do so." Another: "You know that his body was injured. You have a visual image of what he looks like. If you want to see his body tonight, go through that closed door and I will show you how to open the casket. You open it."

Actually, the questions have already been asked by advising that they would be asked later. The responses have been deferred. *Without question, most people opt, given time to consider, to move closer to an experience—to fight, not flee.* I know that because I have tested it for years. People have the courage to move into the pain and experience it now, not later, when given the opportunity. Emotional pain is never a question of "if"—only "when."

Four concepts have been explored through life experiences. *They are depression and helplessness, the fight/flight syndrome, the surrogate suffering syndrome and deferred judgment.* These I use frequently in my funeral practice.

These four concepts are applicable in all phases of the helping professions, be it funeral service, the ministry, social work, medicine, nursing, or in just common old neighboring. *We have gone much too far in America in protecting each other.* We are too far astray in effective helping. Our development of professions and institutions is the most advanced in history, but too many of our policies are for the ease of the professional and the institution to get the job done. *For all this over-protection and interference in human suffering we are extracting an incredible price: the highest level of depressive illness time has ever known.* Hopefully our professions will consider more sensitive and respectful responses to human suffering. *True professionals do not solve problems for others, nor do they protect and shield from truth. They assist others as others solve their own problems.*[1]

After studying these concepts I began to find, in my own work, that the principles that Roy and Tom teach are sound and workable. Our roots have been firmly planted in the soil of grief work. The pioneers who went forth to build a fortress in a desert did not have fake grass to cover the dirt when a loved one died on the plains. The work of burying, as well as building, were everyday realities. Heroic effort was required, which involved spiritual, physical, emotional and intellectual courage. No one ever said, "I don't think I can do this. Would you do this for me?" Everyone shouldered the responsibility for the pain and caught the vision of the promise.

---

[1] Watts, Richard G., *Pastors and the Bereaved*, vol. 4, no. 1, November, 1982. Copied by permission.

On one occasion, while I was giving a workshop in Wisconsin, a woman came who had been a virtual recluse for seven months. She did not leave her home, and no one went in to visit her. I learned in a later conversation that she had given birth to twin daughters seven months earlier. Both of the children died, and when she asked the physician if she could see and hold her little girls, she was strongly advised that seeing the babies was beyond her emotional strength and that she would not be able to "handle it." She asked if she could at least have a photograph of her children and was again advised that the grief process would be easier if she did not look at her children. At that time she was vulnerable and unaware of her own parental rights so she did not pursue the matter of seeing her babies. She told me that she had shut herself away in her home because she had no starting point from which to process her grief. The tools which would have assisted her in that work had been taken away by a well-meaning surrogate sufferer who thought he was doing the right thing.

What would have been a more sensitive and respectful response to her suffering? I have since heard of a new kind of policy operative in some hospitals where parents are invited and encouraged to see and hold their stillborn children or those who die soon after birth. Those parents who refuse to see the babies are given another option. A lock of hair is placed in an envelope along with a photograph of the baby. They are told, "We have your baby's picture on file in our hospital and we will keep it there. If you wish to see it later on, it will be made available to you." Most often, the hospital receives a call weeks or months later, with the parents saying, "We are ready to see our baby now."

A few years ago a tragedy occurred in Utah that shocked and saddened all in our state. A young girl of seventeen and her ten-month-old son were murdered and their bodies were found later in separate locations. Many hearts went out to Roger and Maria, the parents of Carolyn, the young mother, and grandparents of the little boy, Christopher. The body of the little boy was found first, and placed in a cooled area of the funeral home to await the discovery of Carolyn's body so they could be buried together in the same casket. Five days after the baby was found, the grandmother, Maria, petite, dark-haired, and of Greek origin, asked if she could see his body. Maria was told that the baby did not look anything like he did when alive and she was strongly advised not to see him. Nevertheless, in spite of all the negative descriptions, she persisted in her request. Rosie, a member of my family and a friend of Maria's, called me and told me that Maria had been experiencing deep trauma because she had not seen her grandson. I was asked to meet with the couple at the funeral home the following morning. We called the funeral director, and while he strongly discouraged Maria he said we could see the baby.

Knowing the sensitive nature of the case, I called Roy Nichols and asked him if he could advise me about what procedures to follow in my meeting with Roger and Maria. He told me that three conditions would have to be present. (1) There would have to be a desire expressed on the part of family members to see their loved one or an invitation extended to them to do so; (2) They could be given options: Did they want me to look at the body and describe to them what I saw? Would they want to see all of the body or part of the body? Would they like me to go into the room and view the body with them? Did they want to uncover the body or did they want me to? Did they want to be alone or did they want me or a significant other to be with them? (3) They would have to be given time to consider the options.

I met with Maria and Roger at the funeral home the following morning. Rosie accompanied them and seemed to know instinctively how to help them with their grief work, giving positive encouragement by saying, "I know you can handle it. You are strong. You won't be alone."

Roger and Maria had three daughters and Christopher had lived with them in their home. In many ways, Christopher had become like their son. Since Roger had not expressed a desire to see Christopher, I reaffirmed Maria's decision to see the body. I then gave her as many options as I could think of and, using the principle of "deferred judgment," I told her she did not have to make the decision at that moment. She could call me later on or have me meet with her in the funeral home at a later time.

"I have had five days to think about this," Maria said firmly. "I want to see Christopher, and I want you and Rosie to be with me."

We entered the room and Maria uncovered the body. In some cases, where there has been extensive physical damage, the family member may choose only to hold a hand while the rest of the body remains covered. The baby's condition had been explained to Maria, and she chose to uncover the baby herself. After a tender identification was made she asked if we would go and invite Roger to join her for a few private minutes alone. Roger expressed relief that he had been invited to join Maria. A man's response to grief is almost always different from a woman's response. He had not voiced a need to see the baby as Maria had, even though he deeply wanted to be a part of the experience. About fifteen minutes later they emerged from the room and they both said, "It wasn't as bad as we thought it would be."

After I returned home that evening, I received a telephone call. Their daughter's body had been found and they wanted me to speak and sing at a funeral service for both of them. They never expressed regret at having seen Christopher, nor did they have any problems retaining a negative memory picture. Just as we remember a tree in all the glorious seasons of summer, fall, winter, and spring, we remember people we love in the same way.

When Bonnie Bright experienced the death of her husband, Ronnie, she found herself confronted with battles she had never fought before. She learned that grief work was an essential part of the journey ahead of her but that it was not a work that had ever been defined for her. While the promise of eternal life was a great comfort, the mortal task of working through grief was one she needed to do in order to go on with her life. She wrote:

I, like others who have lost a loved one to death, tried desperately to live for the future, to look into eternity, after my husband Ronnie died. Caught between two worlds, I existed in the present but wanted with all my heart to return to the past. At the same time, I tried to focus my eyes upon eternity.

I had been told that God's ways were not *my* ways, but I found grief to be an overwhelming, overpowering, and at times, seemingly unconquerable foe as I tried to find a way to put routine and normalcy back into a changed life, one that would never be the same again. I had not lost my faith in God, nor my desire to move forward spiritually. I had lost my faith in *me*. I desired with all the energy I could muster to give strength back to my family, my friends, my neighbors, and my co-workers. I wanted to give them the peace of mind that I was going to be *okay*, that I had accepted the change in my life and that I would and could go on. But I found myself lonely in the present, unable to cope with changes I couldn't control, and feeling the growing inability to *unconfuse* the confusion caused by grief.

With all the love and help around me, no one remembered to tell me that grief and all the emotional upheaval it can cause are normal and natural parts of loss. About eight months after Ronnie's death, I became involved with a Grief Support Group at Holy Cross Hospital in Salt Lake City, and I made friends with the coordinator of the group, Kathleen Braza. She helped me and others become aware that:

1. I did not have to be *strong* all the time.
2. Tears wash away stress and calm a lonely, wounded heart and soul.
3. I shouldn't fight grief but embrace it and grow from it.
4. Grief has many *gifts* if you work to find them.
5. Grief is natural, but grief work requires a lot of energy, time, and decision-making.

I finally found the greatest of all gifts of grief caused by Ron's death—peace with myself and acceptance of the changes in my life. The burning in my stomach caused by the knife of grief, the loneliness of heart that accompanies death, the confusion of a life in transition are all manageable now, and my spirit has peace and calm as it looks into eternity. But more than anything else, I have regained my faith in *me*.

Bonnie made a significant statement when she said, "Grief work requires a lot of energy, time, and decision-making." There are many persons who, for various reasons, have not had the opportunity to do grief work because they were afraid, or physically removed from opportunities to grieve. When my own father was dying, I found myself involved in three kinds of denial. (1) I did not let my father know that I knew he was dying and over the course of the three months of his illness, we never talked about our real feelings. (2) I was not present when my father died, nor did I attend his funeral service. Afraid of retaining a negative memory picture of my father, I told the family I could not go because I was not feeling well. (3) I did not cry when my father died. I convinced myself I had so much faith in life after death that tears might be an affront to that faith.

It was not until nine years later, after I became involved as a volunteer in a hospital, that I encountered my first dying patient, and began to realize that if I did not help myself to face my own fears and feelings, I would be unable to help others who were dying. I would not be able to walk fearlessly with them through the final moments of their lives.

I met a wonderful grief counselor, Dick Obershaw, from Burnsville, Minnesota, who counseled me and advised me to do the following:

1. Go back in a journal, letter, or verbal experience and say to your father all the things you wish you had said to him before he died. Give yourself the emotional freedom to cry.

2. Do for significant others, indeed for *all* others, what you failed to do for your father. Be present with them in whatever pain they find themselves.

3. Create something beautiful with your grief. Bring all your feelings out into the light and use that energy of grief to create. The song "Teach Me to Die" was a result of my effort to create a musical voice, not only for my father, but for all dying patients. "Teach me to die! Hold onto my hand. I have so many questions–things I don't understand. Teach me to die! Give me all you can give! If you'll teach me of dying, I will teach you to live!"

I now give this same advice to others who have not had the opportunity to "be there" when death or catastrophic illness occurred. Many young people who have come to me seeking help were in the mission field when a loved one died and were unable to return to be with their families. After a recent seminar on grief, I noticed a handsome young man who seemed to be waiting until all the others had left. I stopped putting away my lecture notes and approached him.

"I just returned from a mission in South America," he said. "When I read about this workshop, I knew I had to come. A year before I returned from my mission, my brother was killed in a car accident. He and I were so close. We shared everything growing up together. I wanted so much to come home. Mom wanted me to come home as well, but I wanted to do the 'right thing.' I felt that if I stayed on my mission my faith would be sufficient. I missed seeing my family and being a support to them. I missed seeing my brother in the casket, acknowledging the reality of his death. I missed those talks around the kitchen table where the family laughed and cried as they reviewed wonderful memories they had shared with my brother. I missed seeing the tears on the faces of my friends and feeling their hugs. When I returned home, it was difficult to relate to my family emotionally. It seemed they were in one place and I was in another."

Another young man was on a mission when his mother died. He was encouraged not to come home. When he returned his father had remarried. He was unable to relate to the new family structure, and said he had not been able to go to the cemetery to see his mother's grave.

Many missionaries who had not been present for the grief work have shared similar feelings and some feel a lack of closure years later. Concerned that their own feelings of unfinished grief may be construed to be a lack of faith, some of them have not shared their personal struggles. Those who were encouraged to come home and participate in the experience with friends and family members before returning to the mission field usually express a deep sense of peace and confidence that they made the right decision.

Recently, the hearts of members worldwide were deeply saddened by the slaying of two missionaries. Elder Jeffrey Ball and Elder Todd Wilson were gunned down by terrorists in Lapaz, Bolivia. As the first politically motivated killings of missionaries in memory, the news was shattering. We had just taken Jeff, our third missionary son, to the Missionary Training Center to prepare for his mission to Ecuador, South America. The assassinations occurred the same day Jeff went into the MTC. We were one of countless families to shed tears of grief through the events that followed and the funeral services of these two outstanding young men.

It was a privilege for me to talk with members of both of these families and feel their deep spiritual strength. Jeffrey's father, Brent, told me that his daughter, Wendy, who was serving a mission at the time in Guatemala, was flown to Guatemala City where she could call her family from the mission home. Left in privacy to talk with her parents, she called them.

"Oh Wendy," her mother cried when she heard her daughter's voice, "are you alone?"

"No, Mother," Wendy said quickly. "Jeff is here with me." The feeling of Jeff's presence was a comfort both to Wendy and to her parents.

I asked Wendy how she felt about being with her family during such a devastating time, and she said, "When my mission president told me that Jeff had been killed, I knew immediately I must go home. My family needed me during this time as much as I needed them. It would have taken me a long time to get back into my missionary work if I had not been able to come home. There is a special scripture that says that once you commit yourself to a mission, you don't look back. I'm not turning my back on my mission. Being here with my family was a part of that mission. I did my grief work. I know that they are okay and that my brother, Greg, is all right. And I know that Jeff is all right. We could not have gotten through this without being together as a family, all five of us, because Jeff has been with us too. And we could not have gotten through it without the gospel of Jesus Christ. When I spoke at the funeral service I did it for Jeff. I wanted to tell everyone that even though we don't have Jeff's physical presence, we have his love and his character and his personality, and he is helping us. I knew that I could not tell about his life, but I wanted everyone to feel the kind of person he is. You can't depend on your ears only. You have to listen from the inside and to feel it from the Spirit. Even though Jeff has received a missionary transfer, we need to celebrate his life here."

Wendy returned to the mission field one week following the funeral service.

Laurie Nelson is a beloved friend of our family. While she was on her mission a tragedy occured in her family:

In January of 1995, I had completed a year in the England Mission, and was happily and deeply involved in the work. It was interrupted, however, quite suddenly and alarmingly by a tragic accident which happened near my home in Rexburg, Idaho, involving eight young people, three of whom were my younger sisters. Five Ricks College students, two high school students and one young child were going sledding in the evening of a winter day before school resumed. They were driving on a quiet and lonely highway outside the city limits. The driver of a potato truck traveling on the other road saw the van sliding through the intersection and tried to stop, but the roads were too slick from the sheets of ice, characteristic of the conditions there. Its enormous weight, plus the impact, hit the passenger side of the van. The effects were fatal for five of the young people.

All of these kids were close friends, and three of them were my beloved sisters. Two of my sisters, ages eight and twenty, were among those who died. My eighteen year old sister was a survivor, but she sustained critical injuries.

I was in disbelief, and shock. One sister in critical condition with a head injury, shattered pelvis, and collapsed lungs, and my two sweet sisters dead? I couldn't think straight and clearly. It felt like a bad dream, and I found that the full impact of this news was not being recieved by myself. I was so far away from it all. It was denial I experienced. Others around me cried when they heard the news, but I was too numb. I couldn't even seem to begin grieving for something I didn't want to accept. It was easy to feel this way when I was so distanced from the situation.

It is with much love, respect, and appreciation that I write of a mission president who showed great wisdom and inspirtation on my behalf, counseling me that whatever I decided was right for me to do, he would support. He gave me a choice and asked me to pray for guidance and direction. He had lost a son and knew much of grieving himself. After considerable thought and prayer, I asked him what would happen to me if I went home just for the funeral. He answered that he wanted me to come back. My decision was made, and I've never doubted it since. I felt it was right to go home for the funeral and to be with my parents. they clearly wanted and needed me home during this time. My home teacher arrived at the Idaho Falls Airport to meet me and take me to the hospital to be with my parents and younger sister. There was so much to accomplish. I was asked to speak about my sisters at the funeral. Between hospital trips and visits from relatives, friends and neighbors, there was little time to be idle.

My family spent time in the viewing room with the bodies of my sisters before others came. We prayed, held hands, and knew for ourselves that the spirits of our loved ones were somewhere else. Seeing their bodies was, for me, a powerful relization of this and a final opportunity to express love to the only tangible part of them we had. It all contributed to the healing process for me.

A funeral has an amazing spirit about it when carried out in the right way. What a source of comfort—to grieve openly with loved ones, some of whom had driven far to pay their respects. So many friends and church members had been so gracious, and I truly felt the presence of my two sisters at that special meeting. I gave my talk at the funeral and strengthened many who saw my presence as a missionary at home, a testimony of the importance of the family in God's plan. For me, having the choice to go home and return gave me the tools I needed to begin grieving and start healing, a natural process, which I know has to happen, but for me so far away, wasn't even starting. I was able to put away denial and face the reality, instead of putting it off. I witnessed the pure love of Christ through countless acts of service from neighbors, church members and friends. I felt answers to my prayers, and the prayers of others, in behalf of my parents and surviving sisters during this time when family members are so close and need one another.

Upon returning to England a week later I faced many challenges, but I knew my sisters were cheering me on, and others' prayers were felt. I completed an honorable mission, and I felt happy about this. It was important to me to finish my mission, but I don't know how I would have coped, or what would have happened, had I not come home, or if that opportunity had never been presented. I am grateful for the opportunity to do what I felt was right, and to be allowed to return and complete my mission.[2]

---

[2] Nelson, Laurie. Reprinted by permission.

It may not always be imperative for a missionary to return home when a death occurs in the family. One missionary, whose mother had a terminal illness, knew his mother might not be there to greet him when he returned home. They talked about this possibility, and he was able to make closure and to say his good-byes before he left. When she died, he felt his decision to stay in the mission field was an appropriate one.

Following an accident in her home, my mother almost died before our son, Steve, went to fill a mission in Taiwan. Knowing there was a possibility that Grandma could die while he was away, Steve went to southern Utah where she lived and spent time with her. He talked with her of her past life and brought her a little gift. He knew that if she should die while he was on his mission that he would have felt some closure and comfort in remaining in Taiwan.

The question of whether a missionary comes home when there is a death in the family can be a complex one. There can be important spiritual, financial, and geographical reasons for a missionary to stay in the field. *The most important factor to consider is the agency of the missionary and his or her family.* During a time of death or catastrophic illness, complete freedom of choice should be given to the ones who will be most deeply touched by that loss.

Once the decision has been made by the missionary and his or her family, there should be no judgments made concerning whether the decision was right or wrong. There should never be a subtle encouragement to use faith as a reason to avoid facilitating the important work of grief and loss.

Each missionary should be allowed to return to the mission field of his or her origin, usually within a week. When a determination is made for a missionary to remain in the mission field, there should be a recognition of the loss in the area in which the missionary is serving. I was grateful to learn that in Bolivia the missionaries were able to participate in a memorial service for their beloved companions. At home, the following ideas may be helpful in facilitating the grief work for a missionary. These ideas can also be used for those unable to return because of military service, hospitalization, or financial or geographical limitations.

1. The missionary should be given as many details as possible concerning the death of a loved one.

2. The missionary should be encouraged to put feelings in writing to share the ongoing process of grief in a journal.

3. The missionary should be given an opportunity to pay tribute to the loved one, a tribute that can be read during the funeral service and shared with family members.

4. Video and audio recordings should be made of the funeral service itself. Photographs should be taken and shared.

5. Taped messages from the family and more frequent letters should be sent to assure the missionary that he is not alone and that he is a very real part of the experience, even though he cannot be physically present at the time of loss.

6. The missionary should be given a special blessing that she will be able to not only continue in the work of the Lord, but can use the pain of that loss to create and expand the important work of teaching the gospel.

Health care professionals should remember that when a patient dies in their facility, none of the patient's belongings should be touched without the consent of the family. When my mother died in a nursing home, my sisters and I were promised by the night staff that we could come in the following morning and put away her beloved photos and books, and also the paintings that decorated her walls. We were horrified to come in and find that all her belongings had been stuffed into boxes and that a cleaning lady was waiting outside. I later learned that the morning staff felt they could spare us further suffering if they put away her belongings. It was a classic example of the "Surrogate Suffering Syndrome"! We insisted on going through each box—a procedure that was more painful for us because we had been robbed of the opportunity to gently remove her treasures and fold her clothes. We felt as if our privacy had been violated.

Staff members who are closest to the residents may also have a need to grieve. In some nursing homes, a rose is placed on the pillow and the bed is left empty for a few hours. When there is a recognition of the loss it is a comfort to the family. Meetings held to encourage the expression of feelings of staff members may be helpful. After my mother's funeral I brought bouquets of flowers for the staff, and for the resident who had shared my mother's room.

By way of comfort to those who were not able to be present when a loved one died, I know from experience, that grief work can be done, even in retrospect. The death of my father has taught me important and valuable lessons, and the grief work I had to do for him has not gone unfinished. When my mother died, I was an active participant in her dying process. I was able to give her permission to die—to "go into the arms of love." Assisted by understanding funeral directors, and two of my sisters, I helped to dress her body, fix her hair and sing at her funeral service. I finally learned that *personal involvement* is the key to healing. When we can honor and respect the pain that comes to us in our lives it can become a great resource of creative energy and compassion. As Spencer W. Kimball so eloquently stated, "If we were to close the doors upon sorrow and distress, we might be excluding our greatest friends and benefactors. Suffering can make saints of people as they learn patience, long-suffering, and self-mastery."[3]

---

[3] Kimball, *Tragedy or Destiny*, p.3.

CHAPTER THREE

The Process of Grief

One day a friend, Maureen Bausch, called me from Nebraska. She told me that she had been struggling for some time with a discouraging situation in her life and found it was affecting her family and her work. She asked if I had any ideas that might help her to understand and work through her feelings.

"Maureen, you have two little boys," I said. "Sometimes Chris and Tim go out to play and they fall down and skin their knees. They come to the door crying. Do you appear and say sternly, 'Get out of here and don't come back until you're not hurting any more'?"

She laughed at the thought. "No. The first thing I do is hold them in my arms, kiss their knees, bandage them, and after awhile they go out to play."

"Sometimes when our feelings come to us and they are hurting we try to send them away," I said. "We tell them to stay away until they are not hurting any more. Could you try responding to your sad feelings the same way you would respond to a small child who is hurting? Hold them. Own them. They are your sad children. Allow them to be a part of you. Let me know what happens."

She called me a few days later and said, "Deanna, I didn't have to hold my sad feelings all day. After a while, they went out to play."

I cannot help but believe that the first step we take in the grief process is to make the decision to hold our own feelings in our arms, as we would hold a wounded child. When we stuff them into the attic of our minds or try to hide them in the tiny recesses of our hearts, they may tumble out at the least expected moment, causing us greater pain than when they first appeared. It takes a great deal of courage to recognize and hold our own pain.

Morris L. West beautifully summarized the process of grief when he said,

> It takes so much to be a full human being that there are very few who have the enlightenment or the courage to pay the price. One has to abandon, altogether, the search for security, and reach out to the risk of living, with both arms! One has to embrace the world like a lover, to accept pain as a condition of existence. One has to court doubt and darkness as the cost of knowing. One needs a will stubborn in conflict, but *apt always to total acceptance of every consequence of living and dying.*

Martin Gray said, "We have a powerful strength in us, an energy stronger than a thousand suns. A man's truth is in himself. Sorrow is a good teacher. *He who suffers discovers himself.*"[1]

There are no formulas or recipes to follow when you are processing grief. There are no neatly packaged theories to do a work of the heart. Grief work is heart work, as well as hard work. One of the greatest legacies of Church leader Spencer W. Kimball was a simple two-word sermon: "*Do it.*" He always encouraged us to be about the business of doing now what needed to be done and not postponing our work "until tomorrow." It is easy to postpone our grief work. One of the keys to being involved in the process is to *do it now.*

Just as the pioneers blazed new trails across a wilderness, so we must blaze new trails across the rugged landscape of

---

[1] Gray, Martin, *A Book of Life to Find Happiness, Courage and Hope,* Seabury Press, Inc. from LeLivre de La Vie Editions, Robert Laffont, S.A. 1973, p. 25.

our grief. No one can do our grief work for us. What might be right for one person may not be right for another. There is no "right way" to grieve. No one can tell us how to do our grief work or set time limits on our grief. When we are grieving, it is important to challenge ourselves to take risks with our feelings. When I was teaching in Washington, D.C., one of my workshop participants told me that his father had died recently. He said, "I wanted to know what it was like to see my father buried. So many families do not have that experience because they all leave before the casket is buried. So I took the risk. I hid in the trees and watched them. An indescribable feeling of peace came over me. It was like watching my father being tucked in with a warm blanket of earth."

There may be others who have found it more comforting not to watch the burial of the casket. Once we become pioneers, there will be someone at every turn telling us which mountain pass they think we should take, what clothes we should wear for the journey, and how long they think it will take us. These are well-meaning voices. They all want to help us reach the destination of healing. They all seem to be experts. Sometimes, without meaning to hurt us, they may ask us to let them pull the handcart or guide the covered wagon. They want to protect us. We may even be told that we are not strong enough to make the journey.

When this happens, remember two things. First, keep your faith in God burning brightly. Remember the power of prayer and the wisdom and guidance He has given us in scripture for every circumstance of our lives. Trust in God to walk with you through your journey. Second, believe in yourself. I was in the home of Barry Neil Kaufman, author of the book, *Sonrise*. His little daughter approached me with a note she had written for me. It said, "Don't ask me. Ask *yourself.* Trust yourself." I have never forgotten the power of that message. Look for the light. It is within you!

In an unpublished article entitled, "I'm Going to Do This My Way," Bonnie Bright said:

I, too, am a survivor. I have walked the path of tragedy as I watched death take the "love of my life" and found that I am resilient enough to face tomorrow with the desire to go on, to grow, to learn, and to love with much more consistency, diligence and fewer strings and expectations.

I have grown to understand how emptiness, loneliness, anger, frustration, and guilt can all be part of a healing process, a journey toward wholeness. They are the means by which the hurt can be purged and the loving feelings and memories can bloom again.

I walked the path alone because only I could understand my inner feelings, but I was carried and supported many times by the understanding warmth of family, friends, and faith. I was taught by those who had walked this path before me and encouraged by others who had learned to walk with heartbreak and were willing to hold my hand, give me necessary hugs, ask the yearned-for questions, be willing to share my tears and smiles, and just love me through my journey.

Through time I have grown to understand that this healing process, the journey toward wholeness, the quest to survive, is an ongoing process, not a destination. The mountains of decisions and adjustments become less formidable and overwhelming, and the path becomes easier to follow because the road signs are more legible and prominent. But the growing, learning, sharing, and loving never stop.

To walk with grief as a companion is to go on, not to arrive!

Bonnie's last statement was significant to me because we think it is so important to "arrive" at correct conclusions and to "solve" problems. We want everything explained and every question answered. Perhaps the most frequently asked question when one is grieving is "Why did this happen?" A beautiful response to this question comes with this poem by Ranier Maria Rilke.

Be patient toward all that is unsolved in your heart
And try to love the questions themselves.
Do not seek the answers that cannot be given to you

Because you would not be able to live them,
And the point is to live everything.
Live the questions now.
Perhaps you will gradually,
Without noticing it,
Live along some distant day
Into the answer.[2]

Part of the process of grief work is having the courage to live the questions, without demanding instant answers. Then, and only then, does the concept of "eternal perspective" gain meaning. We cannot see through the eyes of God, but God can see through the eyes of man. In the eternal perspective, He will not leave us without answers.

There are several possible escape routes on the journey through grief that we should avoid: prescription drugs, too much sleep, excessive work, "stuffing" feelings, and delegating grief work to surrogate sufferers. Most people who use drugs excessively in the early stages of the grief process later express regret because in anesthetizing the pain they also anesthetized the love and awareness they needed in those early days of grief. Men have the greatest tendency to use work as an escape. By not spending as much time at home, they avoid collision with memories that full-time mothers must live with every day as they face the constant reminders of their child who is no longer with them. Sometimes the mother who is left at home may escape by sleeping for long periods in the daytime. While this can become a problem if continued too long, the escape of sleep can be healing in the early stages of grief. Wanda Hilton wrote a meaningful poem about her need to sleep after the death of her son Billy.

Sleep beguiles me.
I escape into it. It is like slipping into Peace,
Where I drift in silence,
Unaware of time or space or need or grief.

---

[2] From a letter to Countess Crouy, April 1923.

Sleep beguiles me,
For if I were to dream,
It just might be that I would dream of Thee.
For sleep seems nigh unto that sweet place of being
Where Thou art.
And Thou might speak to me,
Or I might see Thy face.

Sleep beguiles me
For Earth is not so dear
As once it was
Since Thou art gone,
And are not here.

Many studies show that the divorce rate following the death of a child is close to 80%. That number could be vastly reduced if men and women recognized and respected the ways in which they grieve differently.

I recently spoke at the King's College 15th International Conference on Death and Bereavement in London, Ontario, Canada. Dr. John Morgan, coordinator of the conference, has dedicated a great deal of his professional life to organizing these conferences that address multi-cultural and multi-social responses to grief. It is the only conference of it's kind in the world. One of the speakers addressed the major differences between the ways men and women grieve. In his book, *Swallowed by a Snake, The Gift of the Masculine Side of Healing*, Thomas Golden wrote:

The basic differences in the ways men and women grieve lead to dramatically different strengths and paths in processing emotions. Both men and women are affected by our cultural avoidance of death and grief, but this avoidance has a different effect on the two sexes. A woman generally has an easier time dealing with this prohibition in that she probably has a system of support in place in which intimacy is the keyword. This network of friends and family will often encourage the sharing of grief as a means to connect and therefore become more intimate. A man many times has no such system. He highly values independence and autonomy and sharing grief could be a threat to that.

A man finds healing through his grief through "Action" that is harmonious with his need for independence and his orientation towards producing a product. Men tend to grieve in a private and quiet manner. They do not want to "burden" others with their grief.

The fact is, men and women grieve differently. Following the death of a child, for instance, a mother will grieve by crying and talking with her close family and friends. The father, more hierarchal in nature, is more inclined to relate to events through physical action rather than feelings. The grieving father may perform some sort of action such as creating a book, starting a scholarship in the name of the child, or raising money for a special interest the child had. He will want to do something to connect with his grief.

This difference many times leads to misunderstandings. Men and women tend to be suspicious about the other's mode of grief. He may think she is "overdoing it" as she emotes in the presence of those close to her. She may feel that the man is not really grieving because he grieves in private, or through action, not sharing his tears in the same way she does. Yet both styles need to be honored because both, when used effectively, accomplish the same goal—coming to terms with the loss.

Delivering care to men is a difficult task. It is complicated by the masculine tendency towards independence, and societal discouragement of men receiving "help." Once we have an idea of the masculine nature we will see how this nature influences a man's healing.[3]

Giving yourself emotional freedom is essential to healing. The right to laugh and the right to cry are the great facilitating tools in the process of grief. They are of such importance that I have addressed these freedoms in a separate chapter.

---

[3] Golden, Thomas R., *Swallowed by a Snake, The Gift of the Masculine Side of Healing* (1996: Golden Healing Publishing), pp 80-83.

Support groups can be a valued source of help during a time of loss. What a relief to be with and relate to people who have gone through something similar. Compassionate Friends is a national organization specifically for parents who have lost children. Make Today Count was founded by Orville Kelly for people who have life-threatening illnesses. Suicide Bereavement, Seasons Inc., helps with the unique problems associated with suicidal death. It would be wonderful if we could catch the vision of support systems and establish a way to help families who are grieving and who need to meet with others who share their perspectives. After a Church Education Week program in Idaho, many parents who had lost children gathered to talk with me. Soon they were talking with each other. Everyone else had gone home and the janitor was beginning to turn off the lights but we stayed, sharing feelings that had been yearning for expression.

There are many myths of grief and it would be helpful for us to learn to recognize them. Some of them, listed below, have also been identified by Dick Obershaw, founder of the Burnsville Grief Counseling Clinic in Burnsville, Minnesota.

1. *Someday you will get over it.* "Getting over" implies that we should forget, and if grief work is a by-product of our love, we should not try to forget someone we love. While pain is gradually diminished, we do not get over our loved ones any more than our Father in Heaven would "get over" us. In Isaiah 49:16 He says, "I will not forget you, my people. I have carved you on the palms of my hands."

2. *True believers don't cry.* "Jesus wept," emphasizes Dick, and "Jesus was a true believer." An important therapy in the difficult work of grief is the freedom to cry.

3. *Time heals.* If we were to fall down and break a bone and someone walked by and said, "Don't worry. Time will heal you," we might throw a tomato if we had one. It takes work and skill to set the bone into place before the healing

process can begin. Only then, in concert with time, will there be healing. By the same token, our emotional bones have to be set through the grief process before healing can take place. We can be expected to be taken back in time when a sight, sound, smell or voice takes us by surprise! My beloved sister, Miriam, loved red carnations. It is not unusual for me to find tears in my eyes whenever I see a red carnation, even though she died several years ago.

There are many other myths we should examine carefully so that we do not allow the subtle influences of things that are not true to affect the way we grieve.

It is important to be aware of guilt and to have the freedom to acknowledge it. According to the studies of Glen Davidson, guilt basically falls into three categories: (1) Survivor guilt. "Why was it my loved one? Why wasn't it me?" (2) Imaginary guilt. "I wished that bad things would happen, and they did happen." (This is especially true for children.) (3) Real guilt. "Something I did or failed to do caused death or harm to someone I love or to another's loved one." Or "I never said 'I love you' even though I felt it inside."

A child involved in a swimming accident may feel guilty because he was rescued and someone else drowned. A parent may feel guilty when a child dies at a young and vulnerable age before the child has had a chance to experience life fully. Children represent a future legacy, and most parents believe they will preceed their children in death. Imagined offenses or blame—the "if onlys," the "what ifs," and the "I should haves"—characterize the many faces of guilt. Even when the astronauts were killed in the Challenger explosion and when President Kennedy and other great leaders were assassinated, we felt a sense of guilt and helplessness that these things could happen in our country to our own heroes. Our conscience touches us on a personal, national and even global level.

I have heard the phrase, "Happiness is not having what you want. It's wanting what you have." We never fully realize what we have until we lose it. One of the most important personal goals I have is to help people be aware of what they have now, to express love now, so when death or separation occurs, guilt is minimized. It is important for us to recognize guilt and articulate our feelings about it. The admonition "Don't feel guilty" is a useless statement. It is like saying, "Don't have blue eyes." People who are grieving need to recognize guilt, verbalize it, and work toward a resolution of it. We need to realize that guilt can play a positive as well as a negative role in our lives. What I failed to share with my father I have shared in hundreds of hospitals and nursing homes throughout the United States and other countries with patients, residents, and staff members. My guilt has made me more determined to say, "I love you." It has helped me through the creation of songs and through my teaching. When I teach others, I encourage them to examine feelings of guilt and perhaps find a way to create with their discoveries. Here are some of the feelings expressed by workshop participants who were asked to identify their feelings of guilt:

"I felt guilty because I knew Grandpa loved the Christmas lights. I used to pick him up at the nursing home every year and drive him around the city, but the year he died I was too busy. Christmas was a special time for us, but now he is gone."

"My brother and I used to argue about who would get Grandma's possessions when she died. I'd say, 'I want that picture, Grandma,' and my brother would say, 'No, I get it.' Grandma would laugh and say, 'Now you children can fight over all that after I'm gone.' I guess I thought Grandma would live forever, but now that she is gone I don't want her things. I just want her."

"I was the executive of a big company and I was always too busy to take much time with my son. He loved to fish and play checkers, and I would say, 'Listen, son, the reason I have to spend so much time at the office is so I can give you all the things I didn't have when I was your age—a new car, nice clothes, a good college education.' Then my son was killed.

I'll tell you something, Deanna. I would trade my entire business today for one game of checkers with my son."

The sudden illness and death of their youngest son, Jerry, was a devastating blow for the Kocheff family, a happy, active family with five boys. One minute Jerry was playing outside in the sunshine; a few hours later he lay dying in a hospital of an acute infection of the throat, termed "epiglottitis." The morning of the funeral, Jay, the mother of the young child, woke up thinking of all the times she had not fully appreciated the evidence of her little son as he scattered toys and spilled milk. Rather than push aside her feelings of guilt, she began to write them down in a poem called "Play Clothes." I was asked to write a melody to her words, and the song was eventually used in a multi-screen presentation that has been shown throughout the country and has helped many parents to be more sensitive and aware.

Play Clothes

You lie here so still, my little son,
With long dark curls and your play clothes on.
How I wish I could watch you run,
Your soft hair shining in the sun.

How many times I prayed you'd sleep
For one more hour in my busy week
So I could wash or clean or bake
A pie, some cookies or a cake.

How many times did I get upset
When you spilled your milk upon the step,
Or scattered your crumbs on my clean floor,
Or left those smudges on the door?

If only you'd wake in my bad dream
And scatter your toys over everything.
If only I could see you smile
And hold you close for a little while.

Oh God, please forgive all those bad days I had
When I got so upset with this sweet little lad.

Take care of this love while we are apart
And leave his footprints in my heart.

With his curls and smiles, his laughter and fun,
Who lies here so still with his play clothes on.[4]

Once we recognize guilt, we can complete the unfinished business, those things we failed to do for our loved one. The workshop participant who felt guilty about not taking Grandpa out to see the Christmas lights later wrote, "I know I can't take my grandpa now, but I can take someone else's grandpa. Every Christmas I am going to do something to make the holidays brighter for an elderly person!"

There are many ways we can express our unspoken feelings to the person who died. We can do it by writing stories, poems, or songs. We can verbalize our feelings by making a tape recording. We can also write a letter to share our love. Following the death of her brother, Tom, who died in an automobile accident, Kathy Albrecht wrote the following letter:

Dear Tom,

The only regret I have about your death is that I never made it clear how much you meant to me. I'm sure you knew how much I loved you, but I never made it a point to tell you.

You were really a terrific brother. Since you were only one year younger than me, I could really talk to you and share my problems with you like you did with me. Gosh, some of our talks were really deep, and I'll never forget them. Now I have only memories of you, but they're the greatest memories in the whole world.

God almost let you make it to your seventeenth birthday. Your life was only two weeks short of seventeen years. But you really knew how to live. People really had to know you to appreciate your sense of humor, and believe me, I appreciated it when you were around, and you knew it too, didn't you?

---

[4] Edwards, Deanna. "Play Clothes" from the album *Music, Laughter, and Tears*, Rock Canyon Music Publishers, 777 E. Walnut, Provo, Utah 84604.

Of course, I'd do anything to have you back again but I know that's impossible. But I'm sure you're happier now than you would be if you were right here with us today. I surprise myself by thinking that way, but in a way I just can't help but think that's true.

A thought I console myself with is that you'll never have to go through what our family is experiencing right now. Since you were the first to go, all you knew was an alive, happy family. During your whole lifetime, you never had to endure any mental suffering or anguish, which I'm glad about. You're really lucky in a way that God chose to take you first.

Oh, Tom, sometimes I don't know what I'm going to do without you. Every once in a while I get really desperate for you. The pain is unbearable. I know God had a reason for taking you. But I can't help asking, "Why?" Maybe someday I'll find out.

I want to close now by telling you I love you more than words can say. Memories are now the only thing I have. But I'll cherish those memories until the day I die.

With all human love,
Your big sister, Kathy

Those who are grieving are usually advised not to make major decisions such as selling a home or remarrying for about a year following the loss of a loved one. This gives them time to adjust to the changes in their lives. John, a friend of mine, remarried six months after his wife, Jenny, died. Lisa, his new wife, felt threatened by the memories that John still treasured of Jenny. Jealous of a ghost, she removed all evidence of Jenny's life in a home that John had shared with Jenny for many years. Two small sons were permitted to keep only a small photograph of their mother. Before they were able to receive counseling, the marriage dissolved. Lisa later said, "I wish someone had told me how important it was to John and the children that Jenny continue to be a special part of their memories and our lives."

Sometimes pain and despair become so great that facts and theories about grief seem incomprehensible. One day a friend called and told me that, because of recent losses in her life, she did not want to live anymore. Ann had checked into a motel and was considering a drug overdose. I drove to the motel, checked her out, and took her to my home. I found myself discussing all my theories and sharing information that I give in my workshops so I could convince her that life was worth living.

"I've been to your workshops before, remember?" she said.

I suddenly felt totally disarmed, stripped of all the tools I generally use to help others. I said a silent prayer that God would help me find a way to help her. Then I remembered Margaret Snyder, an extraordinary woman I had met during a speaking engagement in Nova Scotia. I had been so fascinated by what she had to say that I had written down a few thoughts and put them with my lecture notes. Margaret had said,

> Deanna, when we laughed and clapped during your program we were not clapping for you. We were applauding because we had been capable of creating within ourselves a moment of joy.
>
> When you welcome a moment of delight—a color, a rainbow, the feeling of warm water running over your hands, a piece of chocolate, the smell of homemade bread—you have created a moment of joy and that moment is alive in you. The animation and the smile that dances on your face are signs that you have created a moment of joy. Empathy is the catalyst of love which stirs you to care and create. The pain of another touches your emotions. You begin to ask, "What can I do, Lord? Help me to help them!" You get an idea and it goes into your hands. Love stirs you up. We are the only creatures capable of creating contagious laughter. We are the only ones of God's creations who can reach beyond this reality. That is why we have altars and funerals. We can celebrate life through our senses, recognize the positive in our environment, and learn to cherish others. When you cherish others, people will not be able to resist you!
>
> Many people believe that faith comes first and joy follows. But perhaps delight comes first, and then faith! Let the earthly pleasures sneak through the back door of your life—the petal softness of a rose, the taste of a fresh strawberry, or the

sparkling eyes of someone you love. The more we actively welcome moments of delight, a sensitivity develops and we are aware of others as we celebrate life.

These moments are as essential as water and food to our bodies. We are nourished by them! *When we are aware of the moments of delight, we are standing in the presence of God.*

I thought this would be a very simple and basic idea to share with my friend. I told her that when we are looking at a landscape there may be beautiful mountains, a forest of pine trees, a cluster of wildflowers on the side of the road, and birds flying about. In the landscape there may also be clump of weeds, a telephone pole or an abandoned old car. If we focus our gaze on the weeds, the pole or the rusted car long enough, it will become the only thing in our landscape. Likewise, if we concentrate only on our despair, it will become the only thing we can see on the landscape of our lives. I asked Ann if she could give her mind a mini-vacation from the pain by concentrating on something else in the landscape for just a few moments. Then she could go back and look at her pain.

I brought her a cup of hot chocolate and asked her to focus on the feeling of the warm cup in her hands and the taste of the chocolate as she drank it. Then we talked again about the feelings that were troubling her. Awhile later, I told Ann I wanted her to focus on something else for about four minutes, and I sang Michael McLean's song, "You're Not Alone."

You're not alone.
Even though right now you're on your own.
You are loved in ways that can't be shown.
Your needs are known. You're not alone.
And when you cry,
You're just letting go a heartache deep inside,
So tomorrow there'll be sunshine and the sky,
And love close by.
You're not alone.[5]

---

[5] Words and music by Michael McLean, © 1983. Shining Star Music ASCAP. Used by permission.

As the evening progressed, I engaged her in animated conversation about some old dolls that were dear to me which, in turn, brought back childhood memories about an old doll in her family. At one point, a look of surprise came over her face, and she said, "We have been talking about dolls for fifteen minutes. I actually looked at something else on the landscape of my life. I can't believe I did that!"

When she went to bed, I gave her a soft teddy bear she could hold through the night and take home with her. Even momentary focus on something comforting, pleasurable, or beautiful can help pull a person out of despair.

It is vital to help a person who is suicidal or in a depressive state of grief to find a support system such as family, friends, a minister, or a therapist. The next day I called a few friends who knew Ann could who came over to offer encouragement. We spent some time that day writing down ideas that would bring us moments of delight when we needed them. Here are some of them:

Study a flower. Touch the petals and smell it.
Have a conversation with someone who cares.
Let the little child in you come alive.
Go outside and play in a meadow.
Make a necklace from dandelions.
Find an old doll or a favorite toy.
Eat a peanut butter sandwich.
Listen to a beautiful song.
Ask someone to hold you.
Go to a good movie and eat popcorn.
Eat your favorite chocolate bar.
Light candles and have a warm bath with bubbles.
Read the scriptures or an inspiring book.
Go to the temple.
Go out and buy something special for yourself.
Take a walk.
Hug a teddy bear.
Do some physical exercise.
Ask someone to give you a back rub.

Look at an old scrapbook.
Bake something.
Each day give yourself an adventure to look forward to!

The wonderful thing about this concept is that when you begin to give your mind mini-vacations from the pain, the vacations get longer and longer. Your eyes begin to linger on the pine trees and you may notice the butterfly darting among the wild sunflowers by the side of the road. The weeds, the old car and the telephone pole are still there, but you are noticing other things on the landscape also. When you are grieving, it may be hard to recognize and "count your blessings." It may be easier just to recognize simple moments of delight. This will stop the pain long enough to give yourself a reprieve, a momentary respite from your pain.

I recently received a letter from Ann. She is doing very well now and sharing moments of delight with others. She said, "I can bear witness that the moments of delight really do work. I don't allow myself to think the same thoughts of despair; I just keep going from one moment to another. Some of my favorites are hot chocolate in my favorite mug, the beauties of springtime, favorite songs, scriptures, temple attendance, and most of all, hugging the teddy bear you gave me. I'm trying hard to live in the peace of the moment, loving and forgiving. The moments of delight are easy."

This simple exercise is easy to practice with children. After the death of a father, a child wrote: "What helped us to get through the 'hard parts?' Friends, sleeping, talking about it, *forgetting about it for little periods of time*, baby brother, writing in my diary, coming to the children's group, and school."

The process of grief also involves reconciliation and forgiveness. We have to forgive the person who died for leaving us with loneliness and unfamiliar responsibilities. We need to forgive ourselves for those acts of omission and commission we suspect hurt the person who died. We need to remember that we did the best we could with the information we had available to us at the time. We need to forgive those who say and do insensitive things. They do not intend to hurt us but they are not acquainted with grief and with the knowledge of what hurts and what helps. We need to forgive others whose carelessness or neglect contributed to the death of someone we loved. We need to forgive the imperfect world in which we live. Without forgiveness we become stuck in the quicksand of the pain and resentment of unresolved grief. But complete forgiveness frees us to remember the beauty inherent in our past relationships and the goodness in other people. It allows us to discover our talents and abilities and to complete our own missions on this earth, and it gives us the ultimate possibility of loving to our fullest capacity! Forgiveness is a treasure twice given. We free ourselves of judgements and resentments, and we free the other person of the pain they feel at having offended us. One of the last great gifts of the Savior was bestowed from the cross.

The Forgiving

Forgive?
Will I forgive, you cry.
But what is the gift, the favor?

You would lift me from my poor place
To stand beside the Savior.
You would have me see with his eyes,
Smile,
And with Him reach out to salve a sorrowing heart—
For one small moment to share in Christ's great art.

Will I forgive, you cry.
Oh, may I—may I?[6]

---

[6] Pearson, Carol Lynn, *Beginnings* (Salt Lake City, Utah: Bookcraft, 1967). Reprinted by permission.

CHAPTER FOUR

What Does Grief Feel Like?

I was busily preparing lunch one day in my kitchen when I heard a knock at the door. I opened it to find my dear friend and neighbor, Wanda Hilton, on my doorstep. Her silver hair framed a face warm with love and expression. I invited her to come in and have lunch with me. As we talked, she shared with me her own struggles with serious illness. Her husband, a member of our bishopric, had been diagnosed with terminal cancer and was undergoing chemotherapy treatments. She was raising a handicapped daughter. Several years previously they had lost a beloved eleven-year-old son in a sledding accident. She had a booklet of poems with her and wanted me to have them. She hoped that the expression of her pain might help others and asked me to use the poems in my workshops and writing efforts. She was afraid if she did not give them to me they would sit in a box in her basement and gather dust. Not long afterward, her husband died. Her own death occurred shortly thereafter. I am grateful to Wanda for her gifts of grief and for her permission to share her great insights with others. She eloquently describes the sacred nature of grief.

The Wonder of This Pain

The wonder of this pain is unlike anything
that I have ever felt before.
I stand in awe of it and know that death
is great and grand

to have such homage paid to it.
It is of God, or it could not strike
so deeply and completely.
It is as near Gethsemane
as man can dare approach
and even then he needs the presence of angels
to bear him up and numb the agony;
the smother, and strangle,
and the cry of it.
The wonder of this pain
is unlike anything
that I have ever felt before.

What does grief feel like? Many of us have already experienced the multitude of emotions and feelings that accompany loss. We can be made more aware of its meaning by walking with others who have suffered deeply and by asking them what grief means to them. The first thing we discover is that the feelings inherent in the grief experience are as vast as man's capacity for emotion. We learn to be nonjudgmental because feelings are not good or bad. Feelings just *are*. We learn that we can never measure faith or depth of love in terms of how a person grieves. We learn to accept feelings as they are, chaff and wheat together. The shock, anger, denial, relief, joy, confusion, sadness, peace, acceptance, longing, tenderness, and anguish and all the human responses to loss are accepted as they are shared with us. Because grief sets us "apart" from others, many feel isolated and have a great desire to communicate with others. The following letters and poems are the eloquent attempts to communicate very real expressions of love and pain.

I wrote a song called "The Littlest Angel in Heaven" for a child, Doug Turno, who was like my own son.

The Littlest Angel in Heaven
The Littlest Angel in Heaven
Loves kittens and cowboys and fun.
Heaven will never be just as it was
Now that his life there's begun.

He'll turn fluffy clouds into snowmen
and swing on the stars up above.
He'll turn golden streets into playgrounds
and fill up God's home with his love.

He'll make dandelions out of sunbeams
and find grassy meadows for playing.
His laughter will ring where the great choirs sing,
But he'll hear me whenever I'm praying.

The littlest angel in heaven
is one I am longing to see
For the child that belongs now with Jesus
Is the child that belonged once with me.

His mother, Carol, wrote the following letter to me after Doug was diagnosed with a malignant brain tumor.

Living with the awareness that your child has a terminal illness is unending madness. From the first moment of learning the odds of survival, your world is shattered. First is shock, then greater sensitivity to writers of philosophy and to all the best in literature. There is a deeper understanding of the grief in every writer's message from the Psalms to Shakespeare, to Teasdale and Edna St. Vincent Millay. After the awareness, though, comes a paralysis, worse than the first shock and grief. The stress goes on for so long that you feel you will break or wish that you would. There is no relief, no place to hide, and no one to pass the cup to for even a moment.

A letter from Karen Wagner was unusually direct in its expression of honest feelings. Excerpts are included here.

Dear Deanna,

My sister said you were interested in learning more about my husband's death. To some people who are not afraid of my feelings I will talk. To others I will not. To you I will talk.

Deanna, our marriage was not always pink clouds and roses, but I loved him, and he loved me and the five kids. We were like a macrame design. Knots everywhere, but a design.

Then we got a call from Carson City, Nevada. They needed someone to build their band. Great. A change was good, and there was a job for me, too. People were accepting, warm, and friendly. Our kids found good friends and we loved it.

When symptoms first appeared, Bill began to get such severe stomachaches he couldn't stand them, so I asked Ann, our oldest, to drive us to Reno. At midnight the surgeon walked out and said, "It doesn't look good. Might be a malignancy." A few days later he told me, "It's no good. It's a bad one—one year at the outside." We ran into blood clots, embolisms, and then came the big decision. The doctor said, "We can buy you time. A special surgery will stop the clots but not the cancer."

At that time I wanted Bill to say "No." A swift death, rather than being eaten away, was uppermost in my mind. I let Bill make the decision. It was his life. So he chose the surgery. Afterward, he couldn't walk well due to phlebitis, but he was home. After several months of therapy and care I saw it coming. Weakening. Vomiting. Hospital again. No more surgery . . . the end was in sight. It was all downhill. I would give him morphine injections every two to four hours and finally hired a nurse the last two weeks of school.

My desk was stacked, the phone rang constantly, I was lost and couldn't function. Got the RN for four hours a day. The night before his death I called a friend. "Please come over for two hours so I can get out of this room!" She stayed all night as I slept.

Next day I knew it was bad, so I called the attending nurse and asked her to come immediately. She and I held his hands until his death. I was frantically praying, "My God, let him fly like a dove, pain free, and full of joy!"

He died, as wished, at home, and I was holding his hand. The memory will haunt me forever, but so will I treasure it. The children were great—scrubbed down the room, cried some and laughed some. "Bet Dad's in heaven starting up a band with the angels!" These kids are great. Crazy, maybe, but great!

How do I feel? How have I felt? End it, end it, end it! "My God, put him and us out of this misery." I feel guilty, lonely, (especially in the mornings), challenged (starting a new life), angry, depressed, all those things. But we had twenty years (come hell and high water), five wonderful children. A new life beckons—he is at last at peace, and now I need to find myself. I hope the kids end up in Japan, Tasmania, or Pago-Pago so I can go and visit them. When moments and hours get rough I remember *my rock*, not sinking in sand. When people say, "Karen, how do you keep smiling?" I say, "A rock." They must all think I'm a geologist.

Our minister has already asked me to assist him in severe cases of emotional problems and terminal illnesses. So we have made it, and so we shall make it. No bell ringing from the bedroom (I still listen for it), no temper tantrums, no dry humor, no two strong arms. But we'll make it!

Death is only a step into eternity. Birth is agony. So is death. Each is a step into infinity. Each one we walk alone, but God is always by our side if only we will stretch out our faltering hands. God has a purpose. He doesn't make mistakes. Our kids have grown and so have I through all this. Six lives touched. The seventh has wings. . . . Learned patience with wife's shaky shots, acceptance of kids' noise, redemption through Christ's love. All is well.

I'm dingy. I start for the west side of town and end up in the east thinking, "I'm really nuts." Went out and bought a $30 suitcase about two weeks before Bill died, got home and said, "Why did I buy this?" Escape mechanism, I guess.

Deanna, I do hope to meet you soon. I dedicate my tear-stained face to you. Whenever I felt I should cry but couldn't, I put on your song, "Teach Me To Die." You made me cry when I needed to.

Cancer: The Stalking Death. Maybe someday I'll write a book titled as such. Cancer gave us anxiety, fear, tears, but time, time for words of love, guilt, apologies, words that needed to be said which all saved us from an asylum, maybe.

I'm haunted forever by my Bill looking like a prisoner from a concentration camp, waking me up at two o'clock in the morning. "My God, my God, why hast thou forsaken me?" He hasn't. *He is there. He is my rock.* Bless you.

Karen[1]

---

[1] Karen Wagner. Reprinted by permission.

Sara King, from Pine Island, Minnesota, wrote a touching essay after the death of her two-year-old daughter, Erica.

What's it like to have your baby die? Not the one you read about while the pages got moist. No, your own. The one it was so painful to think about that you just knew she wouldn't die. When it was someone else's child the tears well in your eyes, but what about your own? The tears in your heart are still dripping, and it's been a month. So what is it like to lose your precious two-year-old? The one you remember with a smile, a "Me, too," a "Yep," and dancing, laughing and singing, smiling and strong-willed.

It's like a sadness you never felt before. One that keeps interrupting your cleaning, your dialing of the telephone, your sleep. It's a vacuum. Not the kind that surrounds you with warmth, but the kind that brings a chill to your blood-stream even without ice cubes. It's waking up in the morning to breathing that isn't there, a voice that cries "Mama" but which is only an imagined echo, a dress still hanging in the closet, idle dancing shoes and a dry toothbrush.

It's looking at the silent snow on icy limbs and having tears in your eyes because you feel just like that. It's going to the supermarket with only one child in the basket and walking down the stairs cradling only one of "my two girls." It's sitting quietly at night with your husband and sharing in silent tears the joy that you wish you still shared. It's laying your heads on one another and just sobbing and sobbing until it seems to dry up for a bit. But that bit is not long, for the tears come again. They come when you meet a friend who doesn't know yet and she asks, "How's Erica?" They come when you wash the dishes and see her favorite yellow bowl used for dry cereal those last days when she wouldn't eat anything else. They come when you find her duck dress in the closet that was her "uniform" last summer. They come when you see other two-year-old children, and her smiling face is not among them. They come when others cry with your loss. They come in happy moments when you look at her picture book, running down to the beach, playing boat in the laundry basket, trying to kiss her sister, or wearing a bowl hat on her head. They come in sad moments when you miss her so much. And they come any moment they please whether you like it or not.

It's hard, but it's not hell. It's not hell because God is here. He has been with us. He has strengthened us, and maybe even cried with us. So, it cannot be hell. But it is not like life either. I look at other people living just like they did yesterday. They are unaffected, unchanged. I want to yell at them, "Don't you know that Erica died?" How can they laugh and go on in their own circles when a bright star in our circle is no longer with us? How can they go on with their petty quarrels and hate for one another, when life is too short, too uncertain, too abrupt? "Oh God," I find myself saying.

"Oh God, what is life all about? Why is love so hard? Why do we love?" I'm not about to stop loving so I will stop being hurt. No, that is not the answer. What is? Is it the eternity picture I forget when I miss Erica so much? Is it because I only know this life and forget that we will be together again "on the other side of the river?" I hope so. I know our Erica is there and that fact tries to warm my heart when I feel so cold. It tries to settle my uneasiness when I wake up early. Someday I may feel it. Today I only know it. Today I say it but some tomorrow I want to live it.

Becky Edwards is a woman who radiates the light within, a light that has been born of tremendous suffering. One sunny day someone came to pick up her children for a swimming outing. There was a car/train collision. Her two daughters and two of her sons were killed. Becky had two surviving sons, Todd and Tom. A few years later Todd needed surgery. Because of improper postoperative procedures, Todd died two weeks after surgery. Becky has one child out of six who survived. She is now involved in Compassionate Friends groups and has helped numerous other parents who have lost children. I have been privileged to have Becky speak at several of my seminars. She is an inspiration to all who meet her. One day I received the following letter from her, written several years after the deaths of her children:

My dear soul-mate, Deanna,

My quiet spare moments are spent at home alone with your music. Such a gift you are to me!

I have to fight through the fog of my anger to find glimmers of God. The knot on the end of my rope is frayed and slipping. My attempts to write you are cluttering up on my table. The emotional expense gets too great to do it all at once. If we lived closer, I could spend hours talking my soul bare and maybe still never get it all said.

I played your songs, "Littlest Angel" and "Remember Me" at our Christmas Compassionate Friends meetings in Emporia and Wichita. We had candlelight memory moments and lit candles in memory of the children we had lost. It was a good time to cry and I found a new "Praise the Lord!" (I really have to hunt for them sometimes.) It was for you and your gift of singing and saying what we feel.

All is not tears here, though we keep the Kleenex Corporation in business. We work at keeping life fun. To some, I can tell it is a relief to them for us to keep it light. But we don't keep it light for the same reasons they want us to. Tom is so good-looking, fun to be with, a delight to my heart, and he could be a total wreck. But despite the depression he wrestles with, he is "pretty much together." We talk a lot. I have to "prime the pump" because it doesn't come all that naturally. The mask of cheerfulness he wears in public makes people think he doesn't have a care in the world. He recognizes the problem it creates, but being sixteen keeps him from changing it much.

I can easily be paranoid every time he walks out the door, but I'm trying to "appear normal," whatever that is. Last Saturday, he was so down, and so was I. I said, "Tom, I wish you weren't so big so I could rock you and make you feel better like I used to do when you were smaller." He said, "So do I, Mom." He sat on the floor in front of me and put his head in my lap and I "rocked" him. He's 5'11" now so that had to do. I'm so glad we can share this kind of love and closeness now.

Todd was demonstrative and every day he would come in and say, "How's it going, Mom?" He would sit and listen and most of the time his arm would be about my shoulder. Deanna, I miss that so much. He really showed how much he loved me. Todd was our natural humorist. He would roll on the floor when something struck him funny. We would end up laughing at him and not the dumb joke.

Brenda would be twenty-four this year. She was tall, long-limbed, with long blond hair—so beautiful for her mere fifteen years. Being the oldest of six matured her early. She was such a natural lady. Her organization around the house amazed people. She used to pray for a little sister, but when Renee was born (last baby, number six), a bundle of sunshine, curly blond hair, bouncy, bubbly, junior cheerleader, aware of her sexiness at three, Brenda was beginning to take all those prayers back because every Barbie case was in order, jewelry box in order, etc., until Renee got hold of it. Renee would be sixteen this summer, a sophomore now, and I look at ball gowns with her in mind. She would be most like me, I think.

Rick would be twenty-two now. At fourteen already he was showing a perfect physique—tall, muscular, and, oh, so handsome, and the girls were "writing notes" daily. He's the one I had to work the hardest to understand. I had an argument with him the day he died. He has been the one I've grieved with more ache in my heart (if one can have more). He was just beginning to assert his decision-making ability.

Brad was another sweetheart, my only child who had brown eyes like my own: shy, curious, a question-asker, a lover who loved to snuggle and cuddle. Larry and I were having marital difficulties when he was little, and I would rock Brad by the hour to make me "feel better." He was the mechanic, the fixer, the scientist. I know he still isn't through asking Noah questions. Brad was shorter, chubbier and so adorable. He would make ladies melt when he would smile. Brad would be twenty now.

Brenda, Rick, Brad, and Renee died August 8, 1976. It seems like yesterday some days. Some days I wonder if that part of my life was really real or did I imagine it all. The part that is buried in the cemetery is the part I bore in my body. Sometimes heaven can't get here quick enough. If I can't act a little like a mother there I'll probably be the first unhappy person in heaven.

Todd died on January 21st, last year. He was a junior in high school, sixteen, and my fourth child. He would be eighteen this May 5th. He would graduate; and it was going to be so much fun.

Your music says so much about celebrating his life; the others, too. I'm determined to do that.

Becky Edwards

So often we take what is most precious for granted. Wanda Hilton expressed this thought in her poem, "If One More Day."

I did not hold you
Warmly close within my arms enough.
I did not cup your sweet child face,
And look deeply in your eyes enough.
I did not smooth your
Soft and ruffled hair enough,
Or listen to your precious words,
Or hear your tumbling laughter.
I did not look upon you
In your quiet sleep enough,
Or kneel and pray out gratitude enough
As I beheld you sleeping thus.
I was not soft, patient, kind,
Indulgent half enough
In my administrations to you.
I do not carry the exact impress of you
Indelibly enough upon me,
In me, through me.
Oh, to have you back
just one more day . . .
My eyes would never leave you.
I would memorize you with every sense,
And repeat you with tender and delicate precision.
I would store up unforgettable impressions
On my very soul
To mitigate this primal loss
If you were here just one more day!

Matt Muldoon wrote a poem that exemplified the fact that we may get over the pain but not the missing.

Like the scent of rain
I don't think about you, sometimes,
For weeks or longer.
Then . . . some pointless dream
Or motherless wandering thought
Will bring you lightly back to me.
Like the scent of rain
Drifting across the desert night . . .
And, like the thirst that grows strong
At the mention of water
A longing wells in me to have
Your soul
Pouring over me again.
And, oh,
I would laugh
And touch you with my joy;
But as the wind carried you here
It carries me away
And I am left dry
Except for the moisture
Your soul has left in my eyes.

My sister, Miriam, lost two sons in infancy. I remember the spring when we were both expecting our first babies. We had been sharing our feelings of excitement for months. Shortly after I had given birth to our first son, their little boy, Bryan, was born. Two days later Bryan died. Michael, another son, died in infancy several years later. She was asked, "Would it have been better never to have carried the children at all than to have lost them?" She responded, "The love that was born within me for my children was an eternal one, and it was worth the suffering because of the assurance they will one day again be mine." Shortly after Bryan's death, Miriam wrote a letter to him:

Bryan, my darling miracle of life, our firstborn,

What a privilege, what a wonderful experience to have our home blessed with your sweet spirit. You came as an answer to many, many prayers, and what an honor to have been chosen as your mother, the woman to have the privilege of giving your body life and nourishment.

When you were one with me, what joys we shared together. You were so active at times and I always knew when you were awake or sleeping and even when you got the hiccups. It was the greatest joy of my life to feel you grow and move inside of me. And what a day when we were finally able to lay our eyes on you! Such a sweet, husky, healthy-looking body. Such delicate hands and feet and what beautiful long black hair. Your eyes were as blue as the skies, and your skin so soft and warm. The sweetest music in all the world was the sound of your first cry and the gusty cries that followed. So pink and wriggly were you. How beautiful to know that we had been partners with God in creating your little body.

Your wee form lies silent now in its tiny blue casket, but your spirit is free and happy and in the very presence of our Eternal Father. It brings your mother and father great joy to know where you are dwelling at this time and to have the sure knowledge that you will live again and dwell with us. Yes, if we live worthily, we will be given the blessing of raising you and watching you grow to manhood.

What a joyful blessing to live for and dedicate our lives to. And so, my dearest, take care until we are one as a family. Always know wherever you are that we love you so very much. Until we meet again.

Mother

Ora Pate Stewart was a writer whom I long admired. When she lost an infant daughter, she wrote an eloquent poem which so tenderly captures a mother's eternal love for her child.

To Glenda

Small as a jewel box is your little casket,
And you, my smallest jewel,

Are treasured up to God within it.
I did not give you willingly . . .
Nor did he snatch you from me.
I rather think the choosing was your own
Or, perhaps, we three had planned together
In some other world
That you would come and make this hasty call,
Then hurry on
That you might light the lanterns on the way
So I could find the footing.
But I have forgotten.
I think you, too, forgot for one brief day.
You tried so hard,
But God remembered;
And then you left me.

I took a comfort in the little clothes
I made so tenderly;
The little petticoat,
The dress, the dainty lace,
The little bonnet
That frames your tiny face,
Your eyes are closed
And mine are dimmed with tears
But maybe you can see with better eyes
And know I love you.

All the dreams we dreamed together,
While you were one with me . . .
These can wait.
I do not count them wasted,
Nor the drops of fresh warm milk
That fall unbidden from my aching breasts
Like beads of pearls unstrung about your neck
And caught by your fixed fingers.
These one day
Will be distilled as manna,
This milk that you have never tasted
Will satiate your soul,
And life will be fulfilled.

Go then my little jewel,
Go back to God.
Tell Him I feel no bitterness at all.
With my own hands I offer you.
I have a treasure laid up in heaven
And where my treasure lies,
My heart will follow.
You are my surety laid up with God.
I will come to you.
I will. I will.
(Ora fulfilled this promise just last year.)

I am often amazed at the similarities of the experiences shared with me by people of many different faiths. In the midst of all the pain there exists another dimension that is often perceived by those who grieve. No matter how horrendous the loss has been there also seems to be a sense of wonder at the sacredness of suffering, an awareness of an intimate presence of God. In the midst of seemingly impenetrable darkness, this awareness can come like a shaft of light when it is least expected. It breaks through human despair and allows the spirit to burn through the darkness and bear witness of the promise that comes with the pain.

There are two occasions when the veil between heaven and earth becomes very thin: when we are born and when we die. When we are holding a tiny baby, freshly sent from God, we have the sense that we are holding a piece of heaven. When we are holding a loved one who is dying, there is often a feeling that we are standing in the presence of God. We become privileged witnesses to the fact that death is not a morbid or fearful event. It is a sacred one. In the same way that we lovingly clothe and care for a baby, newly born, we also lovingly clothe and care for one who has died. Both those dying and those caring for the dying have often shared a sense of the presence of loved ones waiting on the other side, almost close enough to touch.

We can also have joyful experiences at a time of death. This indescribable presence of love and joy was experienced by Betsy Luce, a young mother from Ohio whose husband died suddenly of a heart attack. She wrote:

A profound thing happened to me during the funeral service, unlike anything I had ever experienced up to that point in my life. I suddenly experienced a feeling of peace that is indescribable, and it consumed me and took over my whole being. Then came joy. I felt like a fountain, being filled with love from the bottom and overflowing at the top and constantly replenished. All of these feelings were simultaneous, and it was the most beautiful thing that had ever happened to me in my life.

Charlotte Thomas also mentioned the presence of Christ when she wrote to me about the accidental death of her daughter.

I heard you speak to a group in Seneca, Pennsylvania, last month. My daughter, Cindy, was killed in an auto accident on January 1st of this year. The workshop helped me very much. You asked me what my feelings were after Cindy's death. It is difficult to put on paper exactly how I felt, but I feel I must try to tell you in some way.

The worst part of the whole night was when everyone left and we were alone in the middle of the night with the terrible tragedy that had overcome us.

I remember being alone with my husband in our bedroom and I was trying to console him, being devastated myself. At that time, I suddenly felt the presence of Jesus Christ right there with us. I didn't know how, but I felt that with His help we were going to survive this tragedy. As long as I can remember, I have been a Christian and I believe in Jesus Christ, but I had never felt His presence until that moment. It was such a wonderful feeling to know that He was with us at this terrible moment in our lives.

We miss Cindy so very much. She was such a vibrant, loving young woman, who at nineteen was studying to be a nurse and was so excited about helping people. As you put your arms around me and loved me that night, I realized that love is the answer to our problem. Prior to attending your talk, I wondered how we would ever get through Christmas again. You told about going to the hospital to be with patients. Our family has been thinking about inviting elderly people to dinner with us for the past few years, but we have never done it. This Christmas it will be a reality. Only through helping others will we be able to get our thoughts away from pitying ourselves at this happy season. We know that the spirit of Cindy will be with us and a vibrant part of the whole day.

Cindy's death has certainly changed us, as we are now more compassionate and realize what is most important in this life. I believe in God and am trying to overcome the obstacles that get in my way. God has promised that He will be with us always, and we are holding Him to that promise. With His help there is nothing that can keep us from going forward.

We are trying to remember that promise as we are struggling through our grief. You said that grief is the hardest work you will ever do. It certainly is that. When Cindy's death occurred, I believe she went on into the next segment of life and that heaven is not as far off as many believe. I am confident that some day we will be reunited again. What a joyful reunion that will be! As I have read over what I have written to you, it seems that I have the answers to my questions. Now if only I can apply them in my life. Please hold us in your prayers.

Sharon Kubie, of Pueblo, Colorado, shared the heart-rending story of her three-month-old daughter, Kerry. One day when her baby was teething and crying violently, Sharon tried to ease her pain by rubbing a little aspirin on her gums. The baby suddenly turned blue. She had choked on the small piece of aspirin, and her lungs filled with fluid. Resuscitation efforts brought her back, but she suffered a tremendous amount of brain damage. Sharon wrote:

The first two weeks after the accident, Kerry was in intensive care hanging onto life. Kevin and I felt like King David, who with sackcloth and ashes pleaded with the Lord to spare his and Bathsheba's baby. We kept waiting for a miracle. Slowly, it occurred to us that Kerry might live, but the quality of her life would be minimal.

Kerry has now been institutionalized with uncontrolled seizures and minimal use of her senses. Her spirit is now suspended in a very damaged body. In the last seven months, I had been angry at Heavenly Father for allowing this to happen. But the Lord cannot always protect us from pain. He knows how we feel. He knows of the great pain and anguish we feel when tragedy strikes. He really loves us and I think He would like to prevent all this hurt. I have read many times before how Heavenly Father does not interfere because He wants us to grow from what we experience here on earth. The Lord is not thinking of the moment, but of eternity and our eternal progression.

The Lord has softened my pain. On and off during the last seven months I have felt as if Jesus was personally putting His arms around me and comforting me. I must, however, reach out to God and allow Him in. When I was angry at God and at times unable to pray, I was not allowing the Holy Ghost to comfort me. How hard it is to admit that. This tragedy has succeeded in making Kevin and me realize how much we really need God in our lives and how dependent we are on Him. *Joy is not the absence of pain. It is the presence of God.* Tragedy can increase our joy and increase our faith. I can have my faith added unto, even if Kerry is not made whole in this life. During the Second Coming she will be raised, body and spirit together, and will not be deprived of anything. If Kevin and I are righteous and endure to the end, we will be her parents again.

There is untold human suffering when a little child is murdered. There is horror at the senseless violence that brings about such an act. Parents who have lost a child through violence have an extremely difficult time accepting this hard fact. When a little girl was murdered on her way to school, G. Bradford wrote this poem expressing the possibility of triumph over tragedy.

A Sparrow Fell

A sparrow fell—and no one heard.
Nobody cared. It was just a bird.
From all the numberless flitting throng
Of sparrows, who would miss one song?
But God leaned down and whispered, "I care.
It was one of my sparrows, and I was there."

A little girl, all sunshine and laughter,
(And sometimes scoldings, with kisses after!)
And hurts to smooth over, and deeds to applaud—
A little girl fell! Where were you, God?
A little girl fell! God, why weren't you there?
Is it only for sparrows and such that You care?

If you're God at all—then you could have prevented
This nightmare of pain! So You must have consented.
I've always believed You were loving and good.
I'd like to believe still—if only I could.
But God, if You love me, how can You allow
Such unbearable pain as I'm feeling right now?

Such helplessness—hopelessness—bitter regret—
So many tears that have fallen; and yet
So many more that are still locked inside.
Oh, God—out there somewhere—have you ever cried?
I'm not even sure, anymore, that You're real.
But if You are, God—Do you care how I feel?

*   *   *   *   *   *   *

Beloved, I care! In the midst of your grief,
In the midst of your stricken and crumbling belief,
In the midst of the blackness of total despair,
In the midst of your questioning, Child—I am there.
In the midst! Not far off in some vague fifth dimension,
But there, where you are, giving you My attention . . .

My constant attention—and not just today.
Since before you were born, I have loved you this way.
You're important to Me. Every hair on your head
I have numbered Myself! Can these tears that you shed
Go uncounted? Unnoticed? Nay, child; here I stand

Close enough that each teardrop falls into My hand.
Nor am I a stranger to anguish—to loss.
My own Son was taken one day—by a cross.
I know what you suffer. I know what you'll gain
If you'll let Me walk with you into your pain.
I'll carry your grief, and your sorrow I'll bear.
You've only to reach out your hand—I am there!

Fear nothing for Janet. Your dear little girl
Is safe in My house—and all Heaven's awhirl
With the ring of her laughter, her quick eager smile,
And the things she's saving to show you—"after awhile."
Yes, I could have prevented—but Child, you can't see
With My perfect wisdom. Trust Janet to Me.

Of course you will miss her, but while you are weeping,
Remember, it's only her body that's sleeping.
Her "self" is awake. Wide awake. As I said,
I am God of the living, not God of the dead.
She trusted Me, and My sure Word comes to pass:
"Who believes shall not die." That included your lass.

Let Me walk with you now, through the long, heavy days;
Let Me slowly begin changing heartache to praise.
Take hold of My hand, Child: take hold of My love.
I will lead you to joys that you yet know not of.
Your faith may be weak, and your trust incomplete,
But I'll not walk too fast for your stumbling feet.

CHAPTER FIVE

Is It Okay to Cry?

The Grand Canyon had never looked more beautiful to me than it did that summer. The rainbow colors splashed across the endless canvas of rock and ravine. "Everyone should see the Grand Canyon at least once in a lifetime," I thought to myself as I walked beside a child with eyes of blue and a smile that would melt the ice from anyone's heart. The wind caught his golden hair and tossed it lightly as we approached the swimming pool. Doug hurried to the end of the pool and stopped there, his slight form stretched toward the sun. No one would ever guess he was only months away from death, and neither time nor medicine would erase the tumor growing at the base of his brain.

"Oh, Doug," I cried within myself. "How I wish I could promise you the future, dreams that would come true, and a lifetime of loving!" But I could only promise him this day, this chance to see what everyone should see at least once in a lifetime. And so we made the trip to the Grand Canyon together. He sat with the pilot, and his sister, Megan, and I sat behind in a wind-tossed plane. As motion sickness overcame me, I yearned to make our exit but Doug watched from the cockpit, fascinated with sights he had never seen before. When at last we landed, Megan and I staggered from the plane. Doug picked up our luggage and grinned at us. "I have to take care of you sick ladies now," he said. And take care of us he did. We chased skunks with flashlights at midnight and walked the rim of the canyon at sunset. There was a pool at the motel, and we decided, under the hot summer sun, to take advantage of it.

I approached the edge of the pool cautiously and put my toe into the water. I was never one to run and plunge into a pool. My body seemed allergic to anything cold, and as I tested the icy water I shivered, quite certain that it would take a miracle to get me into it!

That miracle came in the form of a challenge. Doug had been watching me with amusement and with some impatience. He suddenly called from the other end. "I have a great idea! Why don't we jump into the pool together and swim across. The first one across gets a prize!"

I groaned inwardly but responded positively. If he could do it, so could I! I walked over and stood beside Doug. "Ready, set, GO!" he shouted with enthusiasm.

I plunged into the cold depths, icy fingers gripping me as I surfaced, then began to swim as fast as strength allowed. Halfway to the end I heard laughter coming from the edge of the pool, behind me. I looked back over my shoulder, and there he stood, his slender form outlined against the blue expanse of sky. I will always hold him there in my heart and cherish the moment when his laughter filled the air.

"You get the prize!" he exclaimed.

And what a prize. The memory of a little boy who wanted to live until he died! A little boy who was convinced that laughter was life and tears were joy. A little boy who was never afraid of his own humanness.

A physician was once consoling a dying patient who said to him, "I'm not crying because I am dying. I am crying because I never learned to live." Doug lived more in his short life than most people live in a full lifetime. And as he lived, he taught us how to live life fully so that when death came we would never be afraid.

I have learned from dying patients and from those who grieve that laughter and tears are gifts from God to be freely shared. God created us with the capacity for laughter as well as for tears, and did so for good reason. As we share these gifts with those we love, we find that they are interchangeable. We can laugh when we are sad and cry when we are happy as easily as we can do so in reverse. These emotions say, "I love you!" and "I'm so glad to be alive!" They facilitate our healing and brighten the world around us.

Can you imagine what the world would be like if laughter and tears were taken from us? If we could not laugh with delight at a baby's smile or cry when we are deeply moved, how would the world be different? If, at church next Sunday, the bishop said, "Now I don't want to see anyone in this congregation cry when we have our next fast and testimony meeting," how do you think people would respond?

My mother was a single parent struggling to raise a big family by herself. She was practical and hardworking. Born of Norwegian parents, the work ethic had firmly engraved itself on her soul. But work took its toll, and it was rare that she would ever let us see the softness within her heart. That's why I loved to be with Mother in church. Whenever we sang the song, "I Stand All Amazed," I would peek at her from the corner of my eye. "Oh, it is wonderful that He should care for me enough to die for me." The tears were always there, and I loved it. Those were the few times I had a glimpse through the window of my mother's heart.

Elizabeth Field, a gerontologist from Detroit, Michigan, shared with me a childhood experience that brought a smile into my heart!

When I was a child we had a death in the family. A favorite uncle of mine had died. I felt devastated the closer and closer the funeral event loomed. 'What if?' was the key question that stalked me. What if I *couldn't* cry? What would that mean to all the people who knew of my closeness to my uncle? What if they thought I didn't love him as much as they thought I did? I did love him so! I panicked until finally my child's mind devised a plan. I knew from experience that onions made you cry. I instinctively felt I "needed" to cry publicly, so carefully and secretly I hid a slice of onion in my hankie as "grief insurance," and off I went—confident that I had a time-tested prop that would help me be socially correct!

In recent years much research has been done concerning the healing power of laughter. Norman Cousins, during an acute illness, found that laughter does make a difference in the recovery process, and wrote a best-selling book, called *Anatomy of An Illness*, documenting his experience. Some studies show that even the body chemistry is affected in a positive way when we laugh. Many other new studies now document the profound effect that a positive attitude can have on the immune system.

I have learned the difference between laughter that comes from the inside out and laughter that comes from the outside in. Laughter that is artificially stimulated by a T.V. comedian or a funny joke may be expressed only briefly, forgotten quickly, and replaced by a chronic and tired skepticism. But laughter that comes from the inside out is a way of being and believing, like Doug, who was full of light and laughter in the final chapter of his life. It happens best when we allow the little child within us to live—to be our companion even when the years have robbed our bodies of energy and vitality.

When I think of laughter that comes from the inside out I think of the innocent wonder of children and their love for dandelions. Children wait in anticipation for the first dandelions of spring to push their way through the grass. They lovingly pick fistfuls for Mom, have tea parties with the leaves, and sit for hours in a meadow making chain necklaces by fitting the ends of the stems together. They can put them in their mouths to make shredded stems all curly or hold a flower under the chin of a friend to see if the yellow reflection will prove a love for butter or foretell a golden fortune. And when the fuzzy heads become white-haired old men, they close their eyes and blow with all their might. If all the tiny white hairs are gone when they open their eyes, their wish comes true!

Then the children grow up into anxious mothers who view with alarm the spread of dandelions across the grass and irritated fathers about to mow the lawns who bark, "Honey, we've just got to get these darn weeds out of the grass!"

Just as our perspective on dandelions changes as we grow older in our hardened "wisdom," our sense of humor tends to harden as well. Somewhere along the way the wonder and magic gets lost. I love to be around people whose laughter emanates from within like a fresh mountain spring because I know that energy source will be there to help heal the hurt when adversity comes.

And adversity does come. One day in the spring of 1986, I received a phone call from my friend, Father Rick Arkfeld. His very name suggested twinkling eyes and rich Nebraska farmlands. As always his voice was cheerful, even exuberant. "Deanna! I want you to come to my parish here in Randolf. We are going to have a wonderful celebration, and we want you to be a part of it! We need you because you will be bringing our three main ingredients: music, laughter, and tears!"

"It sounds wonderful, Father," I exclaimed. "I'd love to come! But what are we celebrating?"

"I've just been told by my physician that I have lung cancer," he explained. "I may not have much longer to live! I'm so excited, and I wanted to share my feelings with my parish."

"Father, have you lost your mind?" I asked incredulously. "I love you and I don't want you to die!"

There was a moment of silence, and then Father Rick said, "Don't you understand, Deanna, this is a mission, an opportunity to teach people to die with love, with dignity, and with a sense of humor? Are you going to help me or not?"

"I'm coming, Father," I said quickly. "Of course I will come and help you celebrate. You can teach me, too!"

It was a beautiful spring day—a celebration of life. Six hundred people came from the parish and surrounding communities to talk about life and learn about death from a man whose wisdom and humor quickly put us at ease. He said we make ourselves sick by worrying, and laughter is the best medicine to help us face adversity. He shared with us one of his "grave news" stories.

A priest was giving a sermon on preparation for death. At the end of the talk he summarized loudly, "One day every man, woman and child in this parish will die." As a man in the second pew began to laugh, Father repeated solemnly, "One day every man, woman and child in this parish will die." The priest then asked the man in his congregation why he was still laughing. Grinning broadly, the man replied, "I am not from your parish!"

Father told us that he had ordered a fine casket of unfinished wood. He was told by the funeral director that the casket should be finished because it would leave fingerprints if people were to touch it. Father Rick smiled and told them to leave the casket as it was. At his service there will be a big sign that says, "This casket will leave your fingerprints. Please touch."

"Won't it be wonderful," he said, "to be buried with the fingerprints of all my friends?"

He had already chosen his headstone. On one side of the headstone is his serious, theological message: "I will be standing on the bank of the river of death. I'll be watching and waiting to take you home." The funny side says, "I told you I was sick!" He said, "What a delight to know that 100 years from now people will be laughing as they read it! You only die once. Let it be 'you'—your personality!"

As he continued speaking to the group he said, "I decided to be excited about death because I believe that Jesus is excited that I will be coming home again. Death is like a river. On one side of the bank is birth and on the other is death. As we pass through that river we will be totally made well. Death is the most beautiful invitation we will ever receive from God. When we are born into this life, messages of 'congratulations' are everywhere. 'Congratulations! I'm so happy for you!' And so it will be in heaven! When we go home to God we will all be standing tall and looking good in the full knowledge of God's love. He loves infinitely every person He has created! We use so little of our potential in this life. When we are with Him again, our potential will be fully realized. The two most important questions we will have to answer are: (1) Did you love? (2) Did you learn?

"The best way for us to prepare for death is to *live life*! Sell your farm, spend all your money! Go back and live with your kids, and you will all be happy together! If you leave money, they will fight for the rest of their lives!

"There are some people who die at twenty-seven and fall over at eighty-three. They share common characteristics: They hate surprises. What they buy owns them. They don't like noise and dirt. They don't like birthdays. And they don't like little kids. But someday we will all have to break things, spill the milk, put on our play clothes, and go to heaven because only people who are like little kids are going to get there!"

When our laughter had subsided, Father Rick spoke the most profound words of all: "*Fear does not come from God. Courage does.*"

Amidst the circus of autumn colors, in 1996, Father Rick died as my friend and I were on our way to have dinner with him. "You have something more to teach me!" I had said only hours before he died. His last lesson was that we cannot control God, nor have our way through life's vicissitudes. As my friend, Maureen and I, were escorted into his apartment by friends who had been waiting in the driveway for our arrival, we discovered something wonderful! Before being taken to the hospital for the last time, Father Rick had left his hand prints, clearly visible on a thick blue rug. I believe it was his way of saying, "I will not forget you!" I

have carved you on the palm of my hand!" He was a
shooting star streaking across the dark canyon of the sky—
leaving his hand prints and heart prints on all who knew
him.

Father Rick's philosophy reminded me of the following
essay written by Nadine Starr, an eighty-five-year-old woman.

If I had my life to live over,
I'd try to make more mistakes next time.
I'd relax, limber up and be sillier
    than I have been on this trip.
I would climb more mountains, swim more rivers, and watch
    more sunsets!
I would burn more gasoline!
I would eat more ice cream and less beans!
I would have more actual troubles—
    and fewer imaginary ones!
You see, I am one of those people
    who lives sensibly and sanely,
Hour after hour, day after day.
Oh, I've had my moments, but if I had it to do again
I'd have more of them.
In fact, I would try to have nothing else,
Just moments, one after another,
Instead of living so many years ahead each day!
I have been one of those people who never went anywhere
    without a thermometer, a hot water bottle, a gargle,
A raincoat and a parachute!
And if I had it to do again, I would go places and do things
And travel lighter than I have.
If I had my life to live again, I would start barefoot
Earlier in the spring and stay that way
Later in the fall. I would play hooky more often!
I wouldn't make such good grades, except by accident.
I would ride on more merry-go-rounds,
And I'd pick more daisies!

When laughter fills the corridors of our lives, it meets no
obstacles. It is welcomed and celebrated! Tears are usually

given a much less enthusiastic reception. We have heard much talk in recent years about the right to die with dignity in American society. I think it is also time to talk about the right to *cry* with dignity!

During a talk I gave in Canada, I made the statement, "In America, people never die and they never cry."

Before I could explain, several people in my audience said, "Then we're moving to America!"

In America people pass away, pass on to the other side, depart, expire, terminate, kick the bucket, jump in the chariot when it swings low, give up the ghost, and go on to their eternal rest. It is very hard for people to say, "He died." When my son and I were touring England after his mission, I told him I wanted to see if people ever die in England. We were walking through a cemetery near an apartment where he had lived as a missionary. Most of the headstones said, "He/she fell asleep!" A little kid walking through the cemetery in the day time is not going to want to go to bed that night! Look where you go when you fall asleep!

Just as we never die, we never cry. I rarely hear someone say, "She cried." Instead I hear, "You should have seen Martha! She just broke down, fell apart, lost control, and went to pieces!"

One of my favorite scriptures consists of two words: "Jesus wept" (John 11:35). Written in today's modern terminology, that scripture might have said, "Jesus broke down, fell apart, lost control, and went to pieces." When we equate tears with self-pity, unhappiness, weakness, and lack of control, we have passed a negative judgment on one of the greatest privileges of being fully alive and fully human.

One day, when I was visiting Israel, I learned a new meaning of the scripture, "Jesus wept." Our tour guide took us to see the tomb of Lazarus. After descending a narrow staircase, I found myself standing outside the entrance. A brilliant afternoon sun filtered through the opening above us as I stood in awe and remembered that simple scripture. Jesus the man. Jesus the Son of God. Jesus wept. I tried to visualize the Savior as He arrived at the tomb four days after the death of his beloved friend, Lazarus. He had purposely stayed away for a lengthy time "that the Son of God might be glorified thereby" (John 11:4). Planning to call Lazarus forth to life, he looked and saw the tears on the faces of his friends. His heart was deeply touched. He did not say, "Don't cry! Everything's going to be all right!" He simply gifted them with his humanness as He wept with them!

Jesus taught us, not only by what He said, but by what He did. Tears are a by-product of our love and compassion, and even the promise of everlasting life should not strip from us the right to grieve when we experience a loss in our mortal condition. As we hurt, He hurts with us!

> I am a man, but I can cry
> For the fading scent of flowers.
> I am strong,
> But weep my brother's plight.
> I am an ego!
> But I have a soul in search for my Creator.
> I am a man.
> And I will strive,
> But I can also cry.

I sang the song "Take My Hand" for the nationally syndicated talk show Christopher Closeup, which we filmed in New York City.

> Take my hand and walk awhile with me.
> Take my hand and talk awhile with me.
> Just yesterday my strong arms held
> my tiny infant son—
> and yesterday my hands could work—
> my two strong legs could run!
> I was the one with head held high
> and sunlight in my hair . . .

running down a meadow lane—
climbing up the stair!
Take my hand and share with me my fears!
Take my hand and let me see your tears!
Please don't forget to lift your head—
don't let the clouds go by
before you see the forms and shapes
they make against the sky!
Please take good care of all the things
I've treasured day by day—
sunlit crowns on mountain tops!
Rows of new-mown hay!
Take my hand and walk awhile with me.
Take my hand and talk awhile with me!
Take my hand and you will see
the wonders of the world in me!

Through the lowered lights on the set I could see tears in the eyes of our hostess, Jeanne Glynn. "If," she said, "a patient can experience the same sort of release that I just experienced here, *if music can let that happen*, it has a power I never realized before. Crying, in terms of grieving or rejoicing, is something most of us were taught that you do by yourself, or you close the bathroom door and you have a good cry."

"And boys just didn't do it," added our host, Father Dick Armstrong. "So we have all kinds of depressed males walking around who can't cry."

His observation was an accurate one. Men, especially in our society, are expected to be less emotional. When children never see Dad crying, and Mom goes into the bedroom to cry, they begin to think, "There must be something wrong with this." Lynette Olsen wrote me the following note:

When my little girl, Jennifer, was four-years-old, we were watching a sad movie when I happened to look over at her and noticed tears running down her cheeks. She caught my glance and quickly said, "Mommy, I'm not crying. I just drank too much water and now it's coming out of my eyes."

I put my arm around her and said, "Honey, it's okay to cry. That is the way Heavenly Father gave us to get the hurt out."

We are programmed from birth to believe that "big" boys and "big" girls don't cry. Stoicism is mistaken for emotional maturity. Many people in the medical community are uncomfortable with tears. We might hear someone say in a doctor's office, "You were such a brave boy when the nurse gave you that penicillin shot. You didn't even cry!" The inference that he would have been cowardly if he had cried sets the stage for a lifetime of holding in the pain!

A seven-year-old boy was told by an aunt at the funeral service of his father, "Don't cry, son. You're the man of the family now." A double burden was placed on this child. He was told by someone he trusted that he was head of the household at age seven. The second burden was that in this new family position he would not be allowed to cry!

As the mother of four boys, I have recognized a greater responsibility to give my sons the awareness that "great men" cry and that tears can express our joy as well as our pain. I want them always to be comfortable with emotional freedom. On one occasion I returned from a program and learned that our son, Jeff, had cut his head and had to be taken to the emergency room for stitches. Our baby-sitter proudly said, "Jeff was such a big boy when they put in the stitches he didn't even cry." I quickly hugged him and whispered, "If my head looked like your head, I'd cry!" What a blessing to sit recently in our last family home evening before Jeff went on his mission and express our love for each other and cry together.

One day our youngest son, Eric, was climbing his favorite pear tree. It was full of white, fragrant blossoms, and strong branches. However, one of the branches broke and Eric fell to the grass below. He had cuts on his tummy and we took him to the doctor. The doctor said, "Eric, you were such a big, brave boy. I'll bet you didn't cry when you fell from that pear tree, and you're going to be so brave when I fix up these cuts that you're not going to cry now, are you, Eric?"

Very defiantly, Eric looked directly at the doctor and stated loudly in his five-year-old voice, "I did too cry when I fell from that pear tree!" He added with emphasis, "I cried a lot!"

Our society has taught us to associate tears with pain, embarrassment, weakness, and lack of courage. It is not uncommon to hear apologies from those who cry in the presence of others. "I'm sorry," or "Please forgive me," are common statements. From the person who witnesses the tears we sometimes hear, "Don't cry!" or "Why are you crying?" We then feel obliged to share with a stranger or an aquaintance why our eyes are filled with tears.

On one occasion, I was sitting on a plane with an elderly couple seated directly in front of me. They appeared to have lived on a farm because the old man's skin was brown and furrowed, like the earth. After arriving at the gate, the man saw his daughter boarding the plane to escort her aging parents down the ramp. He began to weep tears of joy at the sight of this lovely daughter he had not seen in a very long time. She was both confused and uncomfortable as she lightly scolded him, "Oh Dad, don't cry! Not here! Everything's going to be all right!"

The inference was that everything is all right when there are no tears, but the presence of tears must indicate that something is wrong. The shining gift of trust he had given her was uncomfortably refused. How fine a thing it would have been if she could have cried with him!

Tears do not say, "I'm weak! I'm falling apart! I'm breaking down!" Tears say, "I am a compassionate, sensitive human being. I have a deep capacity to love, and I trust you enough to share my tears with you whether they are tears of joy or tears of sadness!" During a tour of South Africa for Hospice groups, I was asked to perform in a Jewish synagogue in Johannesburg. I was approached by a short, elderly

Jewish man with a crown of white hair. He reminded me of a handsome prince in an ancient castle! He took my hand in his and said, "God gave us two eyes. We cannot cry tears from one eye without crying from another. Out of one eye comes the tears of sadness and out of the other eye comes the tears of joy. *Mix them well.*"

He humbly bent to kiss my hand and then disappeared in a crowd of people. As my eyes searched for him in vain I wanted his kiss to stay on my hand forever! People have given me many wonderful descriptions of the gift of tears:

> "To love is to risk crying."
> "Tears are liquid prayers."
> "Tears are a language only God understands."
> "Tears water the flowers in the garden of the heart."
> "The soul would have no rainbow if the eye had no tears."
> "Great men cry."

Dr. Walter "Buzz" O'Connell, a psychologist and dear friend, said, "The experience of natural lows is essential to happiness. Sharing tears about unwanted endings, unrealized ideals, and insufficient time and energy is practice for your own self-growth. Again no blame, shame, guilt or inferiority complexes over the tears of human compassion. Tears are gifts, not symptoms."

Dr. Glen Davidson, author of the book *Living With Dying*, speaks of the importance of tears, the agent he calls the lubricating oil, the safety valve that so greatly aids in the grief process. This is not to say that one should be compelled to cry because of the expectations of others, but when we continually exert our strength to suppress tears we reject the bonds of trust that could strengthen and support us. We also deny the natural flow of expression of our beings. Some studies suggest the possibility that tears help to drain and eliminate harmful chemicals that are present in the body during periods of grief. Tears also enhance mental health because they enlarge our capacity to feel and to express emotion. My friend Marsha Canterbury Jones has expressed this thought well:

I went through a period of time in my life when I tried to hide inside myself and began to wonder if life was really worth living. When I was able to cry, really cry, I realized that I still had emotions and that I was able to give and receive love. It had been so long since I had felt any emotions besides despair. And I had a friend who cared enough to cry for me. Sometimes I can't cry for myself. It helps to have someone cry for you when you can't.

Christie Lund Coles wrote these two poems concerning the healing power of tears.

Prisms
I have not wept like this in a long time;
I may not weep soon
When this is done,
So, for the moment,
Let me lie here still,
My brief tears forming
Prisms for the sun.

Tears
Weep if you can,
For your grief tears are good.
The grief that gnaws and slowly kills
Has withstood
The stormy crying in the night;
Has watched, dry-eyed,
Dawn's haggard light.

What would it be like to be unable to cry? I had never considered that possibility until I received the following letter.

Dear Mrs. Edwards,
This month I saw your program, at Kettering Memorial Hospital, "Music, Laughter, and Tears." In February 1965, I was a senior in high school. After school, I was in the first car

stopped at a red light. Another car, going the opposite direction, ran the light and hit my car head on. I was thrown back
and forth through the windshield five times. That evening, I
had my brain operated on; the next year, my shoulder; and
the next year, my eye. The eye doctor said my condition was
worsening, and there was nothing else he could do. He
wanted me to see an ophthalmologist and plastic surgeon, Dr.
John D. Bullock, who is known internationally. Dr. Bullock
has operated on me twice. Glass had scraped my eye and
punctured my pupil. There is much muscle and nerve
damage, and my eye is very dry. There is no natural moisture
when I blink, so I cannot cry. I get choked up, my face gets all
screwed up, but no tears. I've prayed and pleaded that I could
cry. Before Dr. Bullock operated the first time, I asked him if
I would be able to cry. Very compassionately, he answered,
"Oh, Trina, I hope so!"
   Sincerely,
   Miss Trina Brander
   Kettering, Ohio

I recently received a letter from Trina. A new surgical
procedure had been performed, restoring her ability to cry.
She wrote, "I'm so excited, Deanna, and I wanted you to be
the first friend to know!"

Other workshop participants have written letters about
how tears have been therapeutic in their lives. I remember
these friends in a very special way. I always smile when I
read a letter that says, "I know you don't remember me. I'm
the one who cried on your shoulder after your seminar!" We
may not always remember the people we laugh with, but we
never forget the people we cry with!

Dear Deanna,
 No words can express the laughter, tears, joys, and sorrows
that fill me right now after listening to you. Death is such a
part of life in so many ways. Although many years have passed
since I've experienced the actual physical death of a loved one,

I have watched as bits and parts of my life have died, my marriage becoming more business than spontaneity, my children more words than part of my being, more desire for quiet than laughter. I'm only thirty-four, but I have been feeling and acting as if I'm 104! Perhaps I had just tranquilized some parts of me. Today, as you shared your experiences, wisdom, and love, I cried and laughed and it felt good and warm! My whole body seemed to swell and I was feeling, *really* feeling! Of course I wasn't the only one. There was much sniffing going on, but today I felt you were there for *me!* Now, the challenge: not to let go again of the ideas and feelings that triggered these responses. I can be happy! It may be a road that has some pain, some risks, some trials, and some uncertainties, but I can make it! Thank you for waking up this "old soul." God bless you.

> Betty Skow
> Kansas

Dear Deanna,

I met you at the workshop you opened last month for Vesper Hospice in Oakland, California. You said I was really "with you" that day. I was, and I did not know why. In fact, I grumbled all the way to Mills College that morning. There were so many things to do at home, so much "business" to take care of. Ten minutes after you entered the room, I knew that you were there just for me. My mind didn't need to be there but my spirit, my soul, was screaming for attention, and you helped me give it what it (I) needed. In the last few years, I have been paying attention (obsessed is more like it) to things that won't matter to anyone in ten years time—mortgages, kids' grades, egos. And I have been miserable. One morning of music, laughter, tears, and a peeling away of layers, and here is Carol. She's all I have to give in this life. *She's enough!* Thank you, Deanna, for helping me find her again. Thank you for helping me recognize her when I did find her. Thank you for shining on my life!

> Carol daSilva
> Moraga, California

Dear Mrs. Edwards,

You probably don't remember me. I heard you at the Pastoral musician's convention. I'm afraid I made a complete fool of myself after your talk last Thursday by crying all over you. I'd like to tell you now what I tried to tell you at the time. I had no intentions of going to your session. I got my rooms mixed up and had planned to go next door. But as you began to talk, I couldn't possibly get up and leave.

When you talked about your father's death, etc., I wanted to leave. A few months ago I was engaged to a guy that I loved very much. We were going to be married this June. One night in March he was in a car accident. I was with him when he died the next day. He told me that he was afraid to die, and no matter what I did, I knew that he would have to die alone. I sang at his funeral, but I never shed a tear. It scared me. I wanted to cry, but I couldn't, not even when I was alone.

As you told your story and I read the words to your song, "Teach *me* to Die," I knew that I had to talk to you, if only to say how much the session had meant to me. If you remember, I couldn't say a word. I just cried and cried for the first time since Joe died.

I can never remember my mother or father ever hugging or touching me. Thank you for hugging me, even though you had never met me before.

> In His love,
> Margie Mehr
> Philadelphia, Pennsylvania

Dear Deanna,

You spoke and sang about a song called "Two Little Shoes" you had written for your little boy. The verse "Each night I kneel, my heart sings a prayer. Thanks, dear God, for one little boy and two little shoes on the stair," touched me because approximately forty-one years ago I lost my first baby. I had a complete layette for our little one. I couldn't touch the baby's little things because I grieved so much, until one day I heard a song on the radio called "Mother, Put My Little Shoes Away." I started crying. I cried and cried and after a long time I dried my tears and I was able to open the closet door where all the baby clothes were. I gently packed them away with my grief, except I saved the two little shoes.

Annabelle Koran
St. Paul, Minnesota

There are many schools of thought in the medical community about what is "professional" and what is not. There are times when it may become necessary to build walls, and times when it is appropriate to allow those walls to come down. I began my music therapy work with a wonderful nurse, Vickie Lannie. Vickie shared a story in one of our seminars that illustrates this point. She had been working with a physician who was rude and abrasive to her and to other nurses, especially when there was an emergency or a "Code Blue." She finally wrote up a report and gave it to her supervisor, telling of her difficulties with this physician. After the report had been shared with him, a wall of silence went up between them. They avoided each other, and when they happened to meet they never spoke to each other.

One day, when Vickie was working in the emergency room, a four-year-old boy was admitted. He had been playing with his dog, and the chain from the dog's neck got caught in the little boy's feet. He was flipped over on his head onto a cement sidewalk and suffered a severe brain injury. The child was dying. Not wanting the child to die on a cold, hard table, Vickie scooped him into her arms and sat holding him. Suddenly she looked down and saw two big shoes in front of her. As she lifted her eyes, she found herself looking into the face of the physician she disliked. The tears were streaming down his face. "I can almost handle it when the adults die," he said. "I just can't take it when we lose the kids."

For him to allow her to see that deeply into his heart took great courage. Several months later, Vickie was admitted to the emergency room where she worked. Some time before, it had been necessary for her to give mouth-to-mouth resuscitation to a patient who was found to have spinal meningitis. They were concerned because Vickie was having severe headaches and consequently was admitted for tests. As she lay in a small room she heard the voice of the same physician. "I heard Vickie Lannie was down here."

"Oh, no! Did he have to pick this time for revenge?" she thought to herself.

He entered her room and said, "It is kind of scary when you are the one going in for tests, isn't it? Don't worry. You won't be alone."

He helped her into her wheelchair, took her hand, and held it the entire time she was being tested. She was found not to have any serious illness, but his presence was a comfort and a strength to her. Now this physician is her favorite doctor.

Tears give patients and staff members alike the message that they are loved and that they will be remembered. When someone comes to us and shares the gift of tears we should never ask, "Why are you crying?" Tears are a very private matter and the one who is crying may wish only to be held, not interrogated. I have found that often someone will cry in my arms after a workshop and will send a letter weeks later sharing their reasons for crying. I received the following letter from a nurse who attended a program I gave.

Dear Mrs. Edwards,

In all your busy schedule, I'm sure you will have difficulty remembering the person who cried after your workshop in Boston, the New England Hospital Assembly. March 31. At first I was going to apologize for my tears but I changed my mind. I simply want to say "thank you."

When I was a senior nursing student, an incident happened I shall never forget. For too many years I have carried around in my heart a picture of a two-year-old child who died as I cared for him. I felt I needed to be "strong" and not "break down," so I carefully buried my tears. Oh, I was kind and tender, but they never knew how I cried inside.

My supervisor praised me for my strength and for not "breaking down." As time passed, I became more stoic. Patients, young and old, died as I held their hands. I knew all the right things to do and say, but no one saw my tears. I kept them carefully hidden.

Even with my own family, I carefully hid my tears. When my two boys underwent major surgery, I was the "rock." When my husband was in Vietnam, I remained "strong." When my two girls cried about leaving friends during our frequent moves, I shed tears for them only inside. When my parents were ill and hospitalized, they never saw my tears. I have cried, but no one ever saw.

Oh, how I have changed my outlook! How wrong I have been! Since your workshop I feel free to cry with others and not to feel "weak." I have never felt so alive and so free! I have become a stronger person! I only hope I can share with others that which you have given me.

Jean Gardner
Sanford, Maine

When I think of the three gifts I want most to give to my children and to those I teach, I think of the gifts that don't cost anything, gifts that will last forever. I shared these thoughts in a song I wrote for my children:

Music, Laughter, and Tears

The toys are all broken you opened last year
And your coat isn't new like before.
Your puzzle is missing some pieces, I fear,
And your train set won't run anymore.
Your teddy is missing his black button nose
And you're tired of the old games we play,
So I have something special to give you, my son,
Don't forget what I'm giving today.

I'll teach you the songs that my daddy taught me
And I'll sing you his soft lullabies.
We'll share all the laughter and joy that we can
And I'll cherish that smile in your eyes.
And if you want to cry when you hear a sad song

Or a story that ends the wrong way,
Please don't be afraid of the tears that God gave.
They will show what your heart cannot say.

I want to give something that never grows old,
Sweet moments to warm you when life is turning cold.
What gifts can I give you to last through the years?
Music, laughter, and tears![1]

In 1989, our world was privileged to witness the fall of the Communism in Europe. Perhaps the greatest symbol of the "Iron Curtain" was the Berlin Wall which separated the Communist and Democratic communities in Berlin, Germany. When I saw a man on a television broadcast, tears streaming down his face, cradling his daughter in his arms as he ran through a hole in the Berlin Wall, I found within myself a sudden desire to go there and see it with my own eyes.

After my arrival in Berlin I met a taxi driver by the name of Richard outside the Berlin train station. He became my tour guide, my financial advisor, and my friend. When we arrived at the wall he handed me a metal hammer and chisel so I could strike my own blows against the wall. As he watched my feeble attempts to make a dent in the massive concrete surface, he suddenly said something very profound: "It's not the walls we build around our cities that represent the greatest dangers to mankind. It's the walls we build around our hearts. To these we must apply the mortal blows that we may know the greater freedom from within." My eyes filled with tears as I realized how often we focus only on the outside freedoms of speech, travel, and the press, and forget the freedoms to laugh and cry and let others know who we really are. I decided to make that my lifelong quest: to come to understand and live the freedom of the heart!

---

[1] Edwards, Deanna, "Music, Laughter, and Tears" from the music album *Music, Laughter, and Tears*, Epoch Universal publications, Phoenix, Arizona, 1978.

When I went back to my hotel room that evening, I wrote the following poem:

The Wall

I stood at the wall with hammer and chisel poised
And threw my might against the metal in my hand.
It would take far greater strength than mine
to loosed bits of concrete from this giant barricade.
It stood, a monument to shame, man's inhumanity to man,
stripped of its power and its name.
I wondered where the blood was shed of those who gave
their lives to cross and conquer it.
Freedom was dearer far than slavery to them,
And we, the benfactors of the price they had to pay.
Rainbow colors crossed it's face.
Some, daring to challenge the arrogance of unrighteous
dominion, had written the words, never to fade from human
conciousness . . .
"WE HAVE THE RIGHT TO BE FREE."
Those vital words were being chipped away,
Soon to be scattered far and wide,
the cry of every human soul inscribed in seven words
upon the ancient page of history!
The tragedy and triumph that it fell before a power greater
than its own!
Could this same structure rise again
if those who held aloft the flame
of freedom were not vigilant?
I saw him standing near the wall with aging face
and greying hair.
An audience he found in me.
I listened to him quietly.
"The greater danger lies not in the walls we build around
our cities, but in the walls we build around our HEARTS!
To these we must apply the mortal blows that we may know
the greater freedom from WITHIN!"

I wish I'd asked him to explain the further meaning of this truth.
He'd lived around these walls for years
and knew the close proximity of freedom and of tyranny.
Was it freedom to lift every man to God,
regardless of his race or creed?
Freedom to affirm the right to be,
the legacy of all humanity?
I knew 'twas my own mortal task
to learn to know the greatest art . . .
to come to know the power of love—
TO LIVE THE FREEDOM OF THE HEART!

CHAPTER SIX

How Do I Know When I'm Healing?

When an acquaintance of mine lost her husband, she was immediately surrounded by a loving and supportive family. Her married children suddenly appeared to talk with her, mow the lawn, cook the meals, and clean the house. Since she had not had such a close relationship with her children for years, she began to depend on her grief to keep her children close to her. The prospect of getting well, in terms of emotional healing and becoming independent again, became a threat to the renewed emotional and physical involvement with her children. So she chose not to get well in order to maintain the constant presence and attention of her family.

Getting well and growing through grief is both a decision and a responsibility. It requires discipline and courage, not so much in terms of feelings as in actions. It is difficult to discipline feelings. But we *can* require action of ourselves. We *can* take responsibility for our own healing process. The help, counsel, and support of others during a time of loss is imperative, but it is wrong to choose to prolong our own pain in an attempt to manipulate and control others.

In the early stages, those who are grieving should be given time to retreat, to "let go," and to stop worrying about meeting the expectations of others and serving others for a time. One grieving person said, "I have to unstring my bow and stop playing the music for awhile." A man whose son was killed said, "Serving others immediately after my son died was like trying to shovel the snow from my neighbor's driveway when I had a broken back." During these times it is right and even necessary for grieving persons to allow others to serve them and to fill their deep needs for empathy and support. But there comes a time when the person who is truly healing will want to "give back" and find a way to serve others in special ways.

There is a difference between "constructive grief" and "destructive grief." Constructive grief will propel us into a process of growth that will give us a deeper spiritual understanding of eternal progression. It will help us to see why there has to be opposition in all things, and we will come to see the benefits of pain in the mortal, as well as the eternal sense.

Destructive grief is the act of internalizing pain to such an extent that we begin to focus only on ourselves and our own needs. Our own needs become so great that we begin to drain the energies and resources of the people around us. Our feelings of low self-esteem can create dependence on the goodness offered us, and foster a subtle resentment on the part of loved ones as they feel the growing needs to get on with their own lives.

Destructive grief can have negative physical as well as emotional and spiritual effects. Dr. Jerome Fredericks, a research scientist for Dodge Chemical Company in Boston, has studied the effects of prolonged grief on the human body. His studies show that unresolved grief can cause high blood pressure, cancer-related illnesses, heart problems, and numerous other diseases. Drug dependence, alcohol abuse, suicide, and depression can also result from unresolved grief. A person whose coping mechanisms include game-playing, dishonesty, or pretense, or who lack self-esteem may find it more difficult to identify and work through unresolved grief.

Before we examine the evidence of healing, it might be well to identify the signs that indicate when we are not healing. People are *not* healing when:

1. *They believe they are victims.*

Victims are always asking, "Why me?" The extension to that question is "Why wasn't it you?" Individuals who feel victimized do not recognize the fragile conditions of their own mortality and the imperfect state of the world. They perceive that bad things are always "happening" to them and that pain is always someone else's fault. Persons who grieve with courage ask the opposite question: "Why not me?" These persons acknowledge vulnerability and the awareness that we live in a world where accidents happen and imperfect conditions exist.

2. *They become dependent on the therapy.*

An unhealthy situation occurs when the therapy becomes more attractive than the cure. The process of employing numerous counselors and attending many therapy sessions over a prolonged period of time becomes a way of life for dependent persons. It becomes a way for the afflicted to receive undivided attention, as continued therapy gives them permission to focus on themselves and their own needs. *These people become walking problems, waiting for someone to solve them.* Friends and family members are often expected to assume the role of therapist. Getting well would mean learning to function independently, as well as serving others. It would mean taking risks and learning to be alone without being lonely. It would take energy and courage to be responsible for their own recovery.

3. *The title of "griever" becomes their identity.*

Dick Obershaw, grief therapist, explained, "Grief is the redefinition of self in relationship to one's life after loss has occurred. When a deep loss is experienced, we have to assume a new identity—that of the griever. Some people may redefine

themselves as 'bereaved' and don't want to change it." Roy
Nichols further explains, "Some people don't want to heal.
No one stays where they are unless it is worth it to them to
stay there." Some people did not enjoy life before the loss
occurred, and they will not enjoy it after a loss. Barry Neil
Kaufman, author of the book *To Love Is to Be Happy With*,
teaches that the reason unhappy people "stay there" is
because they believe that maintaining perpetual anger and
fear is the best way to take care of themselves. He asks a
profound question of those he counsels: "What are you
afraid of?" Once the fear has been identified he asks, *"What
are you afraid would happen if you stopped being afraid?"* It is
a question that would be well for all of us to ponder. Once
we give it serious consideration we begin to realize that fear
does not solve our problems. It only enhances them.

4. *They resort to regressive behavior.*

Dick Obershaw defined this as regressing into perpetual
immaturity, rather than growing toward emotional maturity.
These people avoid being well in the present so they may
assume old identities of the past. They regress into childish
behavior in order to assume less responsibility. A friend
wisely said to me, *"Don't look back too often unless you want
to walk in that direction."*

5. *They participate in activities but do not enjoy them.*

They try to involve themselves in a multitude of activities
but continue to be miserable. They become more miserable
while seeing others around them enjoying life. This is a
normal phase of grief, but if it continues over a lengthy
period of time it can be a destructive pattern.

6. *They live too much in the future or the past.*

A woman whose husband died expressed preoccupation with
wondering what was going on in the next life, and what her
husband was doing there. It was as if she lost the potential for
her own future. Living in the past can also be detrimental. If,

two or three years after the death of a child, the bedroom is still locked, bed and toys are untouched, and clothes are still hanging in the closet, the griever has become stuck in the past because the present is too painful to acknowledge. A good grief counselor would be helpful in resolving that kind of denial. If a grief counseling clinic is not available, there are support groups and books that may be helpful to those who find themselves lodged so firmly in the past that they cannot be happy in the present.

How Do I Know When I'm Healing?

Roy Nichols talks about six principles he calls milestones for healing.

1. *We know we are healing when we can remember and talk about loved ones without so much emotional pain.*

We can begin to talk about them with a freedom and spontaneity that suggests comfort with the memory. Roy points out that this means "most of the time." Even years after death has occurred, a song, a sunset, or a familiar sight may bring tears of emotional pain.

Let me give a simple example that is connected, not to a death, but to sending a son on a mission. The day we took Jeff to the Missionary Training Center was a difficult one for me, but the knowledge of where he was going and what he would be doing filled me with joy. When we returned home, I spent time in Jeff's room, where the only evidence of him was a smiling face on the mirror of his dresser. No tears. I looked through some of his baby pictures and remembered how much I was going to miss him. No tears. Toward evening, when I was straightening the kitchen, I noticed a half-empty bag of corn chips on the cupboard, *cool ranch flavor*, Jeff's favorite! He had eaten only half of them before his dash to the MTC. The tears began to fall freely, and I cried for an hour. During the time he was gone I always experienced an emotional reaction whenever I passed "Cool Ranch Doritos Corn Chips" as I did my grocery shopping!

What a wonderful thing to be able to remember the person without experiencing so much pain! Bonnie Bright said of her adjustment to her husband Ronnie's death, "It is time for a giant step into freedom. Freedom to love the memory but not live with it daily. Freedom to love what I learned from Ronnie but now to go on for graduate studies in life. Freedom to make my choices, knowing that, in the mortal sense, 'we' no longer exist and 'our' decisions are no longer appropriate. Freedom to say, 'I love you' or 'I miss you,' but I don't need you like I used to. Freedom to go on with the assurance that memories soothe the heart, that forgetting pain is a way of forgiving death, and that love has an atomic half-life of eternity, all of which give hope to bad days and add tomorrows for the future."

What Bonnie was saying is that we let go of the "pain," not the "person." Isla Paschal Richardson shared in a poem the importance of remembering the person and not the pain.

To Those I Love

If I should ever leave you
whom I love
To go along the Silent Way,
grieve not.
Nor speak of me with tears,
but laugh and talk
Of me as if I were
beside you there.
(I'd come—I'd come,
could I but find a way!
But would not tears and grief
be barriers?)
And when you hear a song
or see a bird
I loved, please do not let
the thought of me
Be sad, for I am
loving you just as
I always have.

You were so good to me!
There are so many things
to say to you.
Remember that I
did not fear—it was
Just leaving you
that was so hard to face.
We cannot see Beyond.
But this I know:
I loved you so—'twas heaven
here with you!

One of the important cornerstones of the gospel of Jesus
Christ is the commandment to remember. To know is to
love, and to love is to leave your footprints for future genera-
tions. Sometimes, when I am writing in my journal, I
include personal notes to my children and great grandchildren, telling them I think of them often and wish them
much happiness. The faded letters, books, stories, dried roses
pressed between the pages of a journal, all are precious to us.
We want to remember and to be remembered, but there are
times when we will only remember when it is "safe" to do so.
We can talk about a loved one, long since dead, and what
impact their history has had upon our lives. But to risk
talking of someone who died just yesterday or in the recent
past is to risk tears of remembering or to risk seeing the tears
in the eyes of a friend. Why is it so easy to remember Great
Aunt Mary or a great-grandfather when it is so hard to speak
of recent loss? This thought prompted me to write the
following poem, concerning both the past and the present.

Because I Love You

I believe in remembering,
And my memory compels me
To search for you—and find you.
I never saw you smile
Or watched the sunlight

Dancing in your eyes.
You came before me years ago
And opened mortal doors
That I might "be."
You came to earth and gave that gift
Because you loved me.

I want to know you now,
To give you back the gift of life,
To find you on a dusty page
And touch your name with tenderness,
For we belong together,
You and I,
And can be sealed for time
And all eternity.
I remember you,
Because I love you.

I believe in remembering,
And memory compels me now
To speak your name
And hold you warmly in my heart,
Though others turn away
Because they see my pain
in losing you.
My history was written in your name,
For we belong together,
You and I,
And have been sealed for time
And all Eternity.
I remember you,
Because I love you!

2. *We know we are healing when we can experience the full range of human emotions once more.*

Dick Obershaw calls it, "Feeling good about feeling good again." We can begin to react to what is happening around us on a daily basis. We can look at dinner with a friend the night before and say, "I really enjoyed that!"

3. We know we are healing when we can begin to reinvest our emotional surpluses.

If sixty percent of my attention was invested in my spouse and he died, it would be a dangerous thing emotionally to continue to invest that much time and attention in someone who wasn't there any more! Perhaps I could eventually reduce that attention to seven percent in the spouse who died and the remaining fifty-three percent in other people, experiences, and in creative activities. This concept was beautifully stated in an essay written by Bonnie Bright titled: "Welcome!"

But I don't want to go. Please don't make me. It's so scary out there. What if I get hurt again, or someone else dies, or I fall down. Who will pick me up?

What? You say the sky is blue, the trees are green, and it's warm and sunny? The circus is in town? I'm needed? Really? I have something to offer?

Well, maybe I will venture out, maybe just to the end of the sidewalk or the 7-Eleven down the street, or just out to meet the sunshine, the rain, the thunder, the moonbeams, the falling stars, my friends, my new life!

This is similar to how I felt as I made the decision to open the doors, windows, and shades in my house of grief. I say "decision" because to "reinvest" oneself in life takes a conscientious effort. It truly indicates a willingness to face the confusion of living with a determination to make a difference.

It is difficult to open doors and windows that have been your protection and to leave the dust particles of your soul to the mercy of fresh air and light breezes in life. Even though it is refreshing to see the glitter as the sunlight bounces from particle to particle, it is a reminder that life has been somewhat suspended and put on hold while you took care of the personal, selfish, needed business of survival.

Grief pulls the shades on living and darkens a house as nothing else can. We become introspective, self-centered, careful, cautious, protective, bewildered, and reclusive, all to adjust to being "without." In my case, it was being without

my husband Ronnie that made my journey inward so necessary. Getting acquainted with yourself is a frightening corner
in the House of Grief. When all the corners, rooms, and
closets that house your anger, guilt, fear, pain, loneliness,
tears, concerns, decisions, memories, images, responsibilities,
and loves are finally scrubbed and dusted and reorganized,
you feel safe in lifting the shades on the windows and
becoming a part of life again. A time comes when you stop
looking back or down and begin looking straight ahead.

Having invested a lot of time in searching the corners of
our souls, in vacuuming, dusting, and shining the rooms of
our growth and learning—now, maybe now, we can put out
the welcome mat and share the fruits of our labors and make
something worthwhile out of despair. Maybe we can make a
difference because of the tragedy called death and the experience called life. Isn't it wonderful to feel the sunshine?

As I read Bonnie's words, I saw how she had implemented
an important principle. *If you can't change your mind (your
feelings), you can change your methods (your behavior).* Bonnie
did not wait to leave her "house of grief" until she was full of
self-confidence and certainty. She ventured out tentatively—
even reluctantly—but she seemed to know by instinct that
reinvestment in life was necessary; and that, as she did so, she
would be able to see more on the landscape of her life. In an
expanded version of the "moments of delight," she began to
open her life and heart to the world around her. As we
compel ourselves to action, we may find our feelings will
gradually come to be more in concert with our actions.

4. *We know we are healing when our good days begin to
outweigh the bad days.*

We begin to move through our days with the expectation
that some will be painful but many will contain pleasure
and enjoyment. I did not fully understand the concept of
"good days" and "bad" days until my beloved sister, Miriam,
died—then my brother and mother, and others who had
been so significant to me in my life. There did not seem to

be a logical reason for these ups and downs, but—none-the-
less-they were very real!

5. *We know we are healing when we can begin to carry out the
routine of our daily lives in an effective and comfortable manner.*

As with other areas of grief, there are no timetables. For
some it may be a matter of many months before they are
functioning at full capacity in the workplace, in the home,
and in the community; for others it may be a shorter time.
But as comfort levels with life increase, productivity levels in
other areas increase as well.

6. *We know we are healing when we can learn from our
experiences.*

When we are willing to look back, using our hindsight to
prepare ourselves better for another loss in the future, it
becomes a bit like a food storage program. We surround
ourselves with the ability to live and survive in case a loss
renders us incapable of obtaining food in some other way.
Many people know what it is like to be caught in a financial
crisis or natural disaster and not be prepared. How many
have been caught in an emotional crisis and not been
prepared to deal with that crisis because they lacked information and experience? How many of us fail to respond in
an appropriate way, both with ourselves and others, because
we have never been given the tools of survival? Many people
don't have a food storage plan, or a plan to follow in the
event of an emotional disaster because they don't want to
recognize that loss is a part of the human condition. I
remember when the owner of a book store approached me
and said, "I'm not grieving but I read your book anyway."
How important it is for us to study the subject of human
loss and discover the tools we might need in the event that
the landscape of our lives suddenly changes! It would be
helpful to update our wills and discuss with one another
how to help ease the confusion for a loved one in the event
we should die. For example, a husband can write a letter to

his wife detailing the location of important insurance policies and other important documents. The letter could be put in a prominent location that is easy to find.

Whether the wife or a husband manages the financial affairs of the family it would be well to teach the spouse who is not as involved with the finances. A woman may be better prepared if she occasionally mows the lawn or changes a tire. A husband may want to practice doing more of the cooking or household chores normally done by his wife. I would recommend each person writing at least a brief sketch of what kind of funeral they would like to have.

I would like those who know and love me best to participate at my funeral service. I talked with each of my children to make sure they were comfortable with the idea. When my husband expressed reservations, I suggested that he write down the words he would wish to say and give them to his brother or a trusted friend to read.

As we prepare for physical and spiritual survival so we must prepare for emotional survival.

Dick Obershaw says that another evidence of healing is when we can put our memories and emotions into perspective. He points out that where there is a death, the one who dies achieves instant sainthood. It would not be uncommon for a widow to say, "John was the most perfect man who ever walked this earth. He never did anything wrong." A person who went through a recent divorce might say, "George never did anything right. I can't think of one good thing to say about him!" Three years later, the woman whose husband died might say, "John was almost perfect, but, you know, he was always leaving his clothes lying around. I was constantly picking up after him." The woman who went through a divorce might say, "George was a terrible husband, but he sure did love the kids!" Time softens both the idealism as well as the cynicism and helps us to see things as they really were.

When the phrase "Someday you'll be able to do that" becomes "Today I can do it," you know that you are healing.

It is being able to take that first tiny step into the future. As we do, we may find missions ahead of us we can fulfill in a way we could never have done before because we have the courage to walk with pain as a companion. The mission of helping others to heal is a significant and sacred one.

Bonnie Bright is a woman who went from being one of the "walking wounded" to helping others heal their wounds. Today she gives countless hours in service to children who have lost parents, adults who have lost a spouse or a child, and people from every walk of life who have experienced various losses. She is not afraid to walk with victims of Aids, suicide and drug abuse, and has helped to establish support groups within her community to address the very real and practical needs of those who grieve. Healing is her gift, and those who know her have been richly blessed by that gift. It seems appropriate to summarize the concepts shared in this chapter with an essay written by Bonnie entitled "Healing!"

What a wonderful process, healing! It is miracle upon miracle. Have you ever noticed that, as a child when you cut your finger you immediately ran to your mom or dad, and with a gentle kiss and a warm hug the healing process began—pain gone, feelings soothed, energy restored, and life began anew!

As we grow, that process becomes more complex. It then becomes the bandage first, kiss second, gentle hug third, and then, somewhere in the "between," we feel the relief called "healing."

I have a theory. My theory is that healing must start from the inside out, and as a child, the kiss and hug started that process immediately. Everything else, the bandage, medicine, and time was just an inconvenience because we felt first the love and we trusted our instincts that all would be well.

As we grow into adulthood, we tend to complicate this miracle of healing by not loving or trusting as unconditionally, by wanting facts instead of feelings, and by hiding from instead of running toward love first!

The bandage on the cut, the stitches, the cast, the doctor's opinion, or the medical prescriptions are the physical trappings of caring. They close the wound, add security that all that is possible is being done, and, then it is time to run to a loved one for heart-to-heart resuscitation. If the miracle is then believed, the healing process begins—fears exposed, doubts erased, hugs given, pills taken, rest insisted upon—and then a new beginning.

I believe that the healing process after a death follows the very same procedure. It must start from the "inside out" or the wound will become infected and leave a permanent scar.

I was promised, along with others in our bereavement support group, that if we allowed ourselves to feel all our feelings (did not "stuff" them); if we didn't resist our growth ("what we resist persists"), and if we shared our memories, that one day, like the magic of the stitches or cast or medicine, we would find ourselves remembering the person we lost, not with the pain of a hot knife to the stomach, but instead with peace, the peace of a gentle kiss to the heart.

The miracle of healing would then be complete. It would then be time to share ourselves, our memories, our scars, our lives in a new beginning, a celebration of "what will be!"

That promise was fulfilled, and I found my signs of healing to be:

> Decisions without fear,
> Memories without pain,
> Living with energy to spare,
> Loving with smiles to share,
> and beginning—just beginning!

CHAPTER SEVEN

Should We Include the Children?

At Council Bluffs, Iowa, I participated in a workshop sponsored by Make Today Count and Operation Comfort. Both are support groups for the terminally ill and the bereaved. It was the first workshop I had helped to conduct that included children. Children who had experienced the death of a parent, brother, or sister, were assembled for a panel discussion, and all were given an opportunity to tell an audience of approximately three hundred what their grief experiences meant to them.

Supported by their parents in the audience, the children responded one by one, expressing their feelings of loss. At the end of the table sat a freckle-faced, sandy-haired boy about eight years of age. When the microphone was handed to him, he stood, clutching it in his hands. He was unable to speak as silent tears began to run down his cheeks. A friend and I moved forward quickly and took him by the hand, leading him out of the stage entrance through an outside door and into the fresh air and sunshine.

Suddenly our little companion found his voice. "It's my fault my brother died. I killed him!"

We were a bit stunned by the sudden announcement. "How did your brother die?" my friend asked softly.

"Leukemia," the child answered.

"Why do you think *you* killed him?" I asked, amazed that such a little boy could be carrying such a big burden.

"We used to fight a lot," he said, "and when I was really mad at him I would think terrible thoughts. I used to wish something bad would happen to him. Then he got sick and died."

"I want to tell you a story about something that happened to me when I was a little girl," I said. "One day I did something wrong, and my mother spanked me and sent me to my room. She did not like me to talk back to her, so I used my imagination. I wanted to punish my mother because I was angry with her for spanking me, so I imagined a great big fire that burned our nine-room house to the ground. Guess who was in the house when I pretended to burn it down?"

"Your mother?" he asked.

"Yes," I told him. "Then, of course, she would be sorry for punishing me. About an hour or so later, when I began to get hungry, I rebuilt the house, resurrected my mother, and asked her for a peanut butter and jelly sandwich. I forgot all about it until one night my mother went to a meeting. It got very late, and I lay in my room worrying about her. I thought, 'If something bad happens to my mother, it will be my fault because I wished it would happen.'"

"Did something bad happen?" he asked. "Did she come home?"

"Yes, she finally did come home. And when I grew up, I figured out that no matter how angry our thoughts are, they cannot kill someone. I have little boys at home, too, and sometimes they fight so much I can't get a word in edgewise. I think you made the right choice when you decided to fight with your brother."

"He looked at me in sudden surprise. "I did?" He had never thought of his actions as a decision.

"I have been around many children who were very sick," I said. "I have even been with children who were very close to death. Children who are dying want to laugh, play, have fun and be treated like all the other kids. They don't want people to treat them differently just because they are sick. I think your brother wanted to be treated like 'one of the guys.' That was a very special gift you gave him."

A look of instant relief spread over his face. "I wish I could talk like this to my mom and dad, but they don't want to talk about my brother."

"Maybe after today they will," I said, knowing that his mother was in the audience.

As we walked back into the auditorium, I told my new friend he could sit with me for the duration of the program. I wanted to shelter him from pain.

"Not right now," he said firmly. "I have to go back up there and say something to the audience."

I was hesitant, protective. "You don't have to," I whispered. Fortunately, he rejected my efforts to keep him at my side. In that moment he did not need a Surrogate Sufferer!

There was an urgency in his eyes as his little hand slipped from my fingers. "There is something important I have to say."

He looked so vulnerable as he made his way down the aisle and up onto the speaker's platform. A workshop leader handed the microphone to him, and in a loud and courageous voice, the child said, *"I just wanted to say I loved my brother!"*

It was a sermon in a sentence. A hush fell over the audience. We had all become the symbol of his brother. He simply wanted the whole world to know that, in spite of their fights and quarrels, he loved his brother very much.

Should children be included in the process of grieving? The overwhelming response from grief counselors everywhere is this: Tell them the truth! Eda LeShan wrote, "A child can live through anything as long as he or she is told the truth and is allowed to share with loved ones the natural feelings people have when they are suffering."[1]

I was asked on one occasion to sing at the funeral service of a small boy who died an accidental death. Knowing he had little brothers, I found myself looking for them before and during the funeral service. When it became obvious to me that the children had been left out of the experience, I asked a family friend, "Where are the brothers? They should be here too."

"Their mom didn't bring them," she replied, "because she was afraid they would see people crying."

The same little brothers who were left home had probably witnessed untold violence on television in their short lifetimes. The problem with witnessing death and violence repeatedly as "entertainment" is that children never see the process of grief. They never "see people crying." The violence occurs without any mention of the response of moms, dads, brothers, sisters, and loved ones to that loss.

It is also imperative to tell children the truth when a sibling or parent has committed suicide. It should be explained that their loved one did not commit suicide because they did not love the child, but because they were in so much pain. Children should be told by someone they love and trust about the suicide. Otherwise they will get distorted, second-hand information. They should be allowed to be a part of all funeral and memorial services.

The actor, Christopher Reeve, once said of his little son, "My son is a person just like me. He's just shorter."

What if we said to a child, "You can't go to the funeral service because you are too short. You can't go to the hospital to see Mommy when she is sick because only children older than fourteen are tall enough. You can't go to the

---

[1] LeShan, Eda, *Learning to Say Good-bye: When a Parent Dies* (New York: Avon Books, 1976), p. 15.

nursing home because it's depressing to see all those old people." The child is left out of some of life's most significant events.

When a small child's needs are not addressed, a lifetime of resentment can be the result. I was speaking at a conference in Gettysburg, Pennsylvania, when a young woman shared with me a traumatic experience. When her father came to pick her up from her dance class, her little brother, who was in the back seat, opened the car door and fell out into the rush of oncoming traffic and was killed. She remembers seeing the trauma of her father and the blood on his shirt, but nothing was ever explained to her about what happened to her brother. She was immediately whisked off to the home of relatives. When she returned home she saw a picture of her brother on the television set, but there was never any further discussion about him. Later on, when her grandfather was dying, he asked if he could say good-bye to his granddaughter. Believing it would be too much for her, her overprotective parents said "No." To this day her resentment against her parents has not been resolved.

There are two groups in our society we overprotect: the very old and the very young. Amazingly, however, these are the two groups of people who meet death and loss naturally, without pretense, and can teach us how to grieve if we give them the opportunity.

My friend, Mary Obrist, died peacefully of cancer in the early hours of the morning in her home. Her eleven-year-old daughter, Gretchen, was awakened by her father and given the opportunity to spend time with her mother and experience death as a natural part of life. Four-year-old Laura was left asleep until she was awakened by the sounds of morning. She went into the bedroom, crawled up beside her mother, and patted her gently. She was allowed to express her own feelings of grief.

Five days following the funeral service, I visited the family in Lincoln, Nebraska. Their home was overflowing with the presence of Mary. The quilts she had made were draped over chairs, finely stitched pillows lay on the sofas, and rag dolls sat by the fireplace. Flowers from the funeral service decorated tables and corners. Peach-colored roses, Mary's favorite, were beginning to fade. Only weeks before I had been sitting in this same place with Mary, talking with her about how to create a lasting legacy for her children during the final weeks of her illness. She had left evidence of herself everywhere, and had even talked on cassette tapes for Jerry and their three daughters.

Two of her daughters faced me now as I sang the song "For Baby" that Mary always sang to them: "I'll walk in the rain by your side. I'll cling to the warmth of your tiny hand." Laura, dressed in a blue-flowered nightgown, blond curls caught up in pink curlers, placed her face on her soft little arms and began to cry quietly. She was so open, so natural. Clouds of grief left only light showers upon her curls, then disappeared into bursts of sunshine.

"Laura, what can you do to walk in the world for your mommy and celebrate her life?" I asked.

Laura's response came in an instant. "I can plant pretty flowers."

Jerry, Mary's husband, cradled Laura close. "She just planted a honey-locust tree for Mary in our backyard."

"And it's going to grow big," added Laura. She cupped her chin under one hand and rested a dimpled elbow in another as she looked sideways at Gretchen. "What are *you* going to do to walk in the world for Mommy?" When there was a moment of silence, Laura said emphatically, "You *got* to think of something!"

Gretchen's eyes began to twinkle. "We can have a Bavarian Mint Party!" she said. "Mommy ate a whole box of them in the hospital before she died."

I laughed. "My friends are going to have donut parties when I die," I said. "They will bring yellow roses and sing lots of songs. When they talk about all the memories we shared they will probably laugh and cry a lot. It's all right if they cry. I think it would be kind of weird if no one cried."

Gretchen said, "Mommy taught me to sew!" Indeed, her mother, a professional seamstress, had taught many hundreds of women to quilt, and her quilts were masterpieces of meticulous workmanship. Gretchen disappeared and came back with a quilt her mother had finished for her just before her death. I had never seen one so exquisite. I touched it gently and admired the fine workmanship. I turned it over, and in a corner on the back, Mary had written in delicate letters:

"My Dear Gretchen, I love you so much! I started piecing this quilt for you in 1984 and got delayed in working on it with Laura's birth and then Karen's. I got sick in August 1988 and really lost ground on all my projects, but with the help of so many quilting friends it is now finished. I hope you will treasure it forever. With my loving stitches, Mommy."

"This is so beautiful," I exclaimed. "I know something I can do to walk in the world for Mary. I could write about this quilt, and about Mary's creativity and courage, and maybe years from now, it will help someone else."

When we are teaching children about death it is important to use correct terminology. If we do not, they will sometimes correct us. It is not appropriate to say, "She passed away," "He went on to the next life," or "She fell asleep." One of the subtle denials in our society is the term "slumber room" in a funeral home. One day a man going through a viewing line in a "slumber room" looked into the casket at his friend and said, "Oh my, John looks so good! He looks just like he's sleeping." A child standing nearby said quickly, "Nope! He looks like he died!"

I found a wonderful resource in the book *Understanding Death*, edited by Brent A. Barlow. It is a compilation of the writings of authors who give a sensitive and spiritual approach to the subject of death. In the chapter "Addressing

Children," Brent Barlow suggested the following:

1. Explain that all living things die.

2. Discuss death with children before it occurs to someone they love.

3. Making analogies, i.e., "Grandpa is taking a long journey," or "Mom is in heaven in God's garden," can be misleading.

4. Examine carefully reasons given for death. Saying "Grandpa died because he was so old" may make a child believe that other elderly loved ones will die soon.

5. Explain the permanence of death as far as mortality is concerned.

6. Use extreme care in explaining theological implications. A son may wonder why his father was "needed on the other side" when he needs his father right now!

7. Children should be allowed and encouraged, but not forced, to participate in mourning and funeral processes.

8. Parents should do all that is possible to understand and help alleviate a child's guilt.

9. Parents should take time to discuss death with children sometime after the loss has occurred.

10. Initial discussions of death with young children are less threatening if they do not include their own death or that of immediate family members.

Brent Barlow points out that additional theological explanations can teach children about the difference between the spirit and body and the possibility of reuniting of loved ones in a life after death. The concept of a hand in a glove is easy for children to understand. When the body and spirit separate, it is like removing the hand and leaving the glove behind.[2]

---

2 Barlow, Brent A., *Understanding Death* (Salt Lake City, Utah: Deseret Book Company, 1979), pp. 149–151.

There are four basic fears that all children seem to have in common.

1. The fear of "Who will take care of me now?" Children should be assured that they will be watched over and protected by people who love them.

2. Fear of the dark. At a seminar in Canada, an eleven-year-old girl named Suzanne told me her sister had recently died of cancer. She said that just before her sister died she confided to Suzanne that she was afraid of the dark. She had a simple request. "Suzanne, would you be sure to put a nightlight in my casket after I die so it won't be dark in there?" After the death of her sister, Suzanne was taken by her mother to pick out the most beautiful nightlight she could find to put in the casket. In another case, a little girl put her fluorescent dancing shoes into the casket with her brother to bring him some light.

3. Concerns about body position in the casket. One little girl went to the viewing of her grandmother, and the funeral director had closed half of the casket. He had to open it to reassure her that grandma was indeed all there! A little boy in Ohio was taken through the funeral home and allowed to participate in the planning of the funeral service. Shortly before the service began he asked the funeral director, "Did you remember to cross my daddy's legs?" When he was asked why they should be crossed the child replied, "My daddy always used to cross his legs when he lay on the floor to read the paper, and I think he'd be a lot more comfortable that way." He was allowed to do that for his father and was very proud he had been able to put his father in a more comfortable position.

4. Fear of being alone. The fear of being abandoned is a universal fear for children. They do not want to be left alone or to abandon someone they love. Part of their grief work may have to do with reassuring a loved one as well as themselves. A mother took her eight-year-old son to the viewing after his father died of a heart attack. When the child thought no one was looking he slipped something between his father's hands. Mom noticed, and later she lifted up a hand and discovered a wallet-sized picture of her son. On the back of the picture he had written, "You're not alone, Daddy! I'm with you!"

The amazing thing we have learned is the natural way children teach us how to grieve. Elaine Wilson, the mother of Elder Todd Ray Wilson, told us that her family was very touched by a little envelope that came in the mail after their missionary son was killed in Bolivia.

A three-year-old boy had noticed his mother crying after she learned that two missionaries had been shot by terrorists. He asked her why she was crying. She explained what had happened, and that she was crying because she deeply felt the sadness of the families.

He offered her his animal cookies and said, "If you send these to the missionary's mom and dad, it will help them to feel better."

He was right! The cookies did help them to feel better because they were the evidence of a little child's great love and empathy. Sometimes we do not realize the extent and depth of a child's capacity to understand and relate to loss.

In grief counseling, Bonnie Bright teaches the children that "grief brings out all of our feelings. These feelings are all 'okay' and need to be experienced. Just as leaves of a tree are unique and make it one of a kind, your feelings are especially yours to own and grow from and make you one of a kind too!" Children are given a picture of a "Feeling Tree" with all the feelings spelled out on the branches and leaves.

Grief counselors have found that art is a wonderful way for children to express themselves, so in the support group the children are encouraged to draw pictures and write down feelings. Here are some of the feelings expressed by these children:

"No matter what anybody else says, you don't have to forget about what happened. It's okay to remember."

"Try never to say anything you really don't mean."

"Don't be afraid to talk about the person who died. They will always love you forever!"

"I write, 'Daddy, I miss you!' in my diary. Instead of just crying, I write my feelings."

"I felt like my life and happiness were swallowed up. But I also felt a strange happy feeling for my dad."

"Things that helped me when my dad died were to remember that I will see him again, to relax, and not get tense and know it's okay to cry, to talk about it, and know that he will never forget me or my family, and that he will always love me!"

"I handled my angry feelings by skiing, practicing karate, crying hard, riding bikes, and playing football and basketball. When I kept them inside I got sick!"

"You have to think about the good times you had together and talk about what happened."

"When my dad died I was very sad, and this is what I felt like." (He drew a bottle of soda pop bubbling out at the top.) "It is important for me to get over it, talk about my feelings, and not expect Dad to come back. I felt like I was overflowing or exploding, and I felt mad because he wasn't there."

"I didn't like people feeling sorry for me because my dad died, people telling me how I should feel, and some teachers who said I shouldn't feel bad and to keep my mind on my work."

"All day long I felt like I had been hit with a hammer! 'No, don't die! It's too early to leave us! I need your help!'"

"When he first died I thought I would flood the whole house with my tears."[3]

Sandra Fox, in her book *Good Grief,* points out that we have three tasks in helping children to deal with loss. We

---

[3] Bright, Bonnie, and Marcia Nobis, *Grief Through the Eyes of Kids,* Children's Support Group, Kathleen Braza, Bereavement Coordinator.

need to help them understand what grief is, we need to help them understand the process of grieving, and then we should help them commemorate the life of the person who died.[4]

Recently I have been studying the grief needs of children who have been given up for adoption. Many of them try to "earn" the right to be kept with an adoptive family. Without a genetic blueprint or a genealogical road map, they carry a lack of identity and a subconcious fear of abandonment. I am happy to see our society moving toward more open adoptions where family and medical records are given to children, and birth mothers are periodically sent pictures and are informed of how their child is doing.

Monuments are important and kids need to build them. Here are some ideas from the Children's Support Group at Holy Cross Hospital.

1. Do something special in memory of the loved one who died, like plant a tree or a flower.
2. Make something artistic with scissors, crayons, and paper.
3. Write a story or poem, or just write down your feelings.
4. Take flowers to the cemetery on a special day. Put notes in helium balloons and take them outside to a special place and let them drift into the sky.
5. Collect pictures or make a scrapbook.
6. Do something big or do something small. Do something by yourself or do something with others. It doesn't matter at all. Do what makes you feel good!

Another great help for children is music. Teaching children about difficult subjects is a task made easier through

---

[4] Fox, Sandra, *Good Grief: Helping Groups of Children When a Friend Dies*, New England Association for the Education for Young Children, 35 Pilgrim Road, Boston, Mass., 1985, p. 11.

music. During a period of grief they can listen to a song that concerns their feelings of loss, or to special classical music. They can also draw pictures to represent their thoughts and emotions. Children love symbols and colors, so use those tools to help them express their feelings. A visit to the funeral home with a class or as a family home evening activity would be appropriate. Enlist the help of a sensitive knowledgeable person to explain the purpose of funerals.

Give children the opportunity to help each other. Children have expressed the need for a "compassionate friends" group for kids and not just for adults. So often we attend only to the grief needs of adults and we fail to address the issues of what the losses mean to children. In a previous publication, I shared an example of the importance of children helping other children. Doug Turno, the little boy who was dying of a malignant brain tumor, was sent to Oregon where it was hoped he could be a candidate for new experimental treatments with chemotherapy. Because of the extensive progress of his disease, it was decided that Doug could not be a candidate for treatment. As soon as he began to realize that he had only a short time to live, Doug turned his attention to other critically ill children on his unit in the hospital. He would seek the children out and spend time talking with them. One of the patients he paid particular attention to was a little boy named Johnny. Johnny had a brain tumor like Doug's but he did not have the strong love and support system that Doug had. His parents were divorced and because of the pain involved in seeing him so ill, they rarely came to the hospital. Because of their deep fears, the parents were relying on the staff to become Johnny's surrogate family. Johnny had become withdrawn and lay quietly in a darkened existence, not smiling, not eating, and not involving himself in activities.

Then one day Doug quietly entered Johnny's room and spent time with him. After their visit, there was a noticeable difference in Johnny's attitude. He began smiling again. He was hungry. He wanted to go for rides in his wheelchair.

During my last visit with Doug, in his grandmother's sunny kitchen in Aiken, South Carolina, I asked him what he had said to Johnny that had made such a difference. Both Doug and I seemed to sense it would be our last meeting. We had shared so much and been through so much together. But "so much" is never enough when you have to say good-bye. I knew I could not leave Doug without knowing more about the secret conversation that had helped give Johnny the will to live. I could not go until I was Doug's student one more time.

I placed my arm around his shoulders and put my face next to his. Decadron treatments had caused his face and cheeks to swell almost beyond recognition, but nothing had changed his enormous lashes and soft blue eyes. "Doug," I whispered, "before I go, I just want to know what you said to Johnny when you first visited him in the hospital. What did you say that made such a difference? I don't want to pry, but I think I can learn something from you about how to help other children like him."

Doug was modest as he reached back to recapture their conversation. "Oh, I didn't say much. I just told him I knew how he felt because I had a brain tumor just like his. I told him if he had any unfinished business or work that he needed to do, I could help him do it." A mischievous smile crept over his face. "I told him the nurses didn't like it, but I had lots of candy bars hidden in my room, and I would share some with him whenever he got hungry."

The smile vanished as he searched for the rest of their conversation. "Oh, yes, I told him that sometimes I felt like crying, and if he ever felt like crying, he could come into my room and we could cry together. The last thing I told him was, 'Don't be afraid to die, Johnny. I'm not afraid.'" Then he hesitated as he confessed, "To tell you the truth, Deanna, I am kind of scared, because I've never had any experience."

My breath caught in my throat. I held Doug close to me, awed by his wisdom and insight, and the gift of himself that he had so freely given to all of us. No psychiatrist on earth could have helped Johnny as well as Doug had helped him.

We can help children to be more sensitive to grief by recognizing and acknowledging the great and small losses in their lives. Children go through many traumatic experiences: the loss of a beloved pet, the impact of divorce, the loss of self-esteem, moving away from a best friend, or the physical death of someone they love. As we respect their pain, they will grow into a deeper awareness and respect for the pain of others.

I was very moved by a father who took time to address a loss experienced by his little daughter, Paige, when her pet parakeet died. James A. Goodman, Waycross, Georgia, wrote the following:

To Paige, on the loss of your pet.
With love and sympathy, Dad.

Ode to "Pepper"—Late Resident Parakeet

I'll miss you, "Pepper," though you and I didn't get off to a great start. I hope you didn't take it personally. I would have been against any bird being brought into the house.

Pepper, I never knew one little bird could make so much noise, create such a mess, require so much attention, and so totally captivate a family.

You were a real performer. I was always amazed at the versatility of your repertoire; your splendid soaring arias, your melodic warbling, your romantic rhapsodies—pity you couldn't tell time! You were perhaps most noted for your rasping screech against some real but mostly imagined travesties, of "your space." Look, bird, I now understand and do apologize for the time I innocently dangled that coiled black headphone cord too near your cage, but why did my flipping the newspaper send you into orbit?

The classics were your favorites. You liked Dvorak's Symphony #5, Opus 95 most of all, and the Eurythmics' "Love Is a Stranger" least! One thing about you—you weren't afraid to express your opinion!

You were a narcissistic little thing, and I thought you would wear that mirror out kissing and preening in front of it for hours on end. This led to speculation that you would just love to have some company in that cage.

Remember the cute way you welcomed her by placing your left foot on her precious breast and shoving her right off the top perch?

It's funny how all that biting and sparring never drew any blood. And, yes, we noticed how the beak-to-beak biting began to last a little longer and to be accompanied by quiet little comments between you two. I thought she was pretty, too, Pepper. We called her Sunshine, but I always wondered what your name for her was. She will be fine; we put her in Paige's room to comfort both her and Paige last night. It seemed to help.

I thought it a real tribute when Paige demanded through her sobs that you be buried in one of her socks when she saw that I had placed you in one of mine.

We buried you in the prettiest part of the front yard, near Paige and Sunshine's window in the shade of the old provider cedar. I thought you'd like that.

Paige learned a lot from you, my little friend. She learned a lot more about certain things than I alone could ever have taught her. I'm grateful to you for that.

You taught her that it's okay to state your opinion, to sing along with that which you like, to complain loudly when you feel threatened, to bite back if you absolutely must, to be wary of strangers but to love freely if they prove worthy of that gift. Your short life had much meaning; God knew where you were needed. Even your death was a lesson. Paige has tasted the bitter tears of your passing, and she will be better for it, understanding that life is a gift from God, and it is to be appreciated while it lasts.

I'll miss you, Pepper, and as I was gently placing your spent little body in that diminutive sock, I wished, selfishly, that you would again bite me, but you and I both know that in a far greater way you have done just that![5]

Children also make good counselors when we give them the chance. When my sister Miriam died, it was my

---

5 James A. Goodman. Used by permission.

youngest son, Eric, who cried with me so I would not feel alone. He suggested that I leave a tape of the music we had sung together in Miriam's casket. A child's feelings, concerns, and questions can only be addressed by allowing them to participate in the process of grieving. In return, they will help us to deal with our own feelings of loss.

One of the most beautiful expressions concerning the needs of children came in the form of a poem written by Bonnie Bright:

Please Don't Overlook Me!

I know my size is smaller
> my hands are littler
> my legs are short,
but my HEART
> can hurt just like yours.

I'm a CHILD
> You're an adult . . .
> Please don't overlook me!

I know my vocabulary isn't the greatest
> my attention span lacks longevity
> my logic sometimes seems irrational,
But my MIND
> can question death just like yours can.

I'm a TEENAGER
> You're an adult . . .
> Please don't overlook me!

I know my needs seem less important
> my feelings seem less controlled
> my actions are hard to understand,
But my BODY
> needs a hug just like yours does.

I'm YOUNGER
  you're older . . .
Please don't overlook me!
I know tears are hard to show
  fears are difficult to face,
   death means not coming back,
But my SOUL
  searches for reassurance just like yours does.

*I'*m HURTING
  And you're hurting, too . . .
  Please don't overlook me![5]

---

[5] Bonnie Bright. Used by permission.

CHAPTER EIGHT

How Do I Help a Loved One?

A moving story was told in the *Reader's Digest*, condensed from *Guideposts* magazine. Madge Harrah shared how one quiet act of kindness helped calm her storm of sudden grief. She had received a call from her hometown in Missouri telling her that her brother and his wife, her sister, and both of her sister's children had been killed in a car accident. "Come as soon as you can," her mother begged. Madge and her husband were in the midst of a move between states, and their house was in total confusion. Her husband made plane reservations for their family to leave the following day. Still in a state of shock, trying to manage the needs of her own two small children, she sank down on the couch and surveyed the unfinished tasks before her. Her doorbell rang, and she opened it to see a neighbor standing on the porch. "I've come to clean your shoes," he said simply.

Confused, she asked him to repeat. "I remember when my father died. It look me hours to get the children's shoes cleaned and shined for the funeral. So that's what I've come to do for you. Give me all your shoes, not just your good shoes, but all your shoes."

She said that the image of Christ's presence symbolized by a quiet man kneeling on her kitchen floor with a sponge, a pail of water, and the shoe polish sustained her. Now, whenever she hears of an acquaintance who has lost a loved one, she no longer calls with the vague offer, "If there's anything you need, let me know." She tries to think of one specific task she can do such as cooking a meal or taking the children for a few hours. She reaches out to give one gift, the gift of herself. If she is asked, "How did you know I needed that done?" she replies, "It's because a man once cleaned my shoes."[1]

On one occasion, I was in a hotel van being driven from the airport in Pittsburgh. I was weary because of a hectic schedule and wanted nothing more than to lie down in the seat behind the driver and rest. She began talking incessantly, and I was annoyed because her conversation necessitated some response from me. Suddenly, she began to tell me that her sister's two small daughters had just been killed in a car/train collision on their way to school. I sat up abruptly, as if I had just been moved into another state of consciousness. I began to ask questions and to listen carefully to her answers. I wanted to know about her sister and whether she had a strong support system. As we were nearing the hotel, I said, "If you can stop for a few minutes I have some music for your sister. I want you to give it to her for me, and I hope the songs will be helpful."

When we are touched by the pain of another, something within us is called forth to respond to that loss. The promise of comfort given by the Savior is kept through us: our hearts, our hands, our gifts. Each one of us has different talents, and God uses those talents to comfort others. It does not matter so much what we give as it does that love is communicated through the gift. One may give the gift of a freshly made loaf of bread. The Wilsons received the gift of animal cookies from a three-year-old. Because the music I create is a part of my heart, that is one of the gifts I give when someone is hurting. Even when we do not know the

---

[1] Marrah, Madge, "I've Come to Clean Your Shoes," *Reader's Digest*, Dec. 1983, p. 21.

family, it is appropriate to offer help. We may feel helpless and impotent but can simply ask if there is any way that we can be of service to run errands, clean a house, or help with the funeral service. Rarely will sincere offers of help be rejected or go unappreciated.

Whenever I hear someone say, "I hope I never have to endure pain like that," I think of the song, "No Man Is an Island." How true it is that each person's joy is our joy and each person's grief is our grief. Pain is never far away from us. It becomes a reality to me when I hear of 236 people dying in a plane crash. When there is an earthquake, war, or starvation in some part of the world, I feel the loss. When the lives of millions of unborn children are discarded because their presence is "inconvenient," I grieve inside. When I think of the holocaust of a war where six million Jews died, I mourn that this happened in my world, in my lifetime. Something stirs my heart when the silence of a summer afternoon is broken by the anxious voice of a siren, because I know that someone else is hurting. Empathy is the capacity to feel the pain of another, the struggle to come nearer to an understanding of the process of grief. When pain is not happening to us directly, it is happening to countless others around us. If we did not love deeply, we could never feel the pain. Love is what enables us to reach out, to give, and to serve. To love is to commit ourselves to the service of our fellowmen.

All of us want to know how better to help someone who is suffering, whether it is a distant friend or a member of the family. I receive many letters from people who ask me how they can help someone they love. One woman wrote:

> Our son died in a rather traumatic manner, and to this day my husband has never talked about him to anyone. He has told me that he has many guilt feelings about things that happened over the years before our son's death, and he just cannot talk about it. As a result, I find myself curling up inside but longing for that sharing of grief and feelings with

my husband. Although our life on the surface seems very happy, we can never be truly close until we can work through this situation. I feel I have worked through my grief over the years except for the longing to be closer to my husband. How can I help him?

Sometimes it is only a simple recognition of pain that helps another person. When someone really listens and tries to comprehend, or gives another the opportunity to talk about it or helps a friend to cry for a loss they have kept bottled up inside, it can make all the difference. A man who attended one of my classes said, "My son died seventeen years ago, and today I was able to cry for him for the first time."

Another young woman, Dawn Star Fire, from Mission, B.C., Canada, tucked a little poem she had written into my pocket. These little gifts of the heart give me the energy I need to continue to serve others.

> I want to take a moment from the softness of this day
> To say a special thank you before you go away.
> I cried so many tears as I listened to your words;
> All the things I've tried to say that no one's ever heard.
> My brother died last fall and the pain was all too real,
> But no one wants to hear of death or how you really feel.
> When he died I couldn't cry. I refused to even face it.
> But denial didn't change my loss or help me to erase it.
> So many months of silence and existing in a vacuum,
> Released now by a stranger's voice I heard across a room.
> Free for the first time to feel the loss and pain,
> And in the freedom of these tears I know I'll laugh again.
> When my circle is complete and I greet the joyous end,
> I'll remember you, Deanna, as a very special friend!

Nothing brings more joy in this life than helping to ease the pain of someone who is suffering. It takes a desire to risk walking closely with someone who is wounded so we can involve ourselves in a process of giving and receiving. We all have gifts to give and lessons about life to teach one another.

What are some of the ways we can learn to give of ourselves more freely and openly? Perhaps the first step is to ask grieving persons what they need. Only from them can we receive the information needed to minister effectively to those who walk in the dark forest of suffering.

I met a man in Omaha, Nebraska, named Vern Albrecht, whose sixteen-year-old son died in an automobile accident. A chaplain from the Lutheran Medical Center, he shared his thoughts in an article titled "Helping Families Face a Tragic Death."

Three years ago something happened in our family that you read about almost daily in the news as happening to someone else, but not to you. Our oldest son, Tom, and his girlfriend, Lynn, were killed instantly in a head-on automobile accident. Tom's death was exactly two weeks before his seventeenth birthday. He was a senior honor student at Central High School. Lynn was also sixteen. She was a junior in an all-girl Catholic high school.

There is really no way I can fully describe the impact and hurt this tragedy had on me, my wife and our other five children. Nor is this the intent of this paper. Suffice it to say, there is no pain we have experienced so far in life that is in any way comparable in its intensity to that of Tom and Lynn's untimely deaths. How can you help families face tragedy such as ours, or those even more tragic, such as lingering deaths, multiple deaths, shootings, stabbings, suicides, burnings, or whatever?

First, you need to know how it feels. It hurts! It really hurts! It hurts each member of our family individually and together. We cried a lot. Alone. And together. We felt guilt! Why didn't we do some things differently? Why did I wait until Tom was gone to tell other people how proud I was of him? Why didn't I tell him every day how glad I was to have him as my son? At first we felt a sense of numbness. We felt a sense of unreality, but it was real. Our little ones handled some of their feelings by making paper caskets and patching up torn papers with scotch tape—papers that were ripped apart in imaginary auto accidents.

Some of the calls and letters from friends and people we had never met who had gone through a similar experience really helped. The understanding love they gave us can't be overstated! Some of my previously negative feelings about the greeting-card industry changed as hundreds of cards came in, each one giving a little life.

Do you have to experience these things personally before you can understand them and be of help to others in similar situations? I do believe that personally entering and experiencing the "dark valley of loss and grief" can be of great help in understanding the pain of others who are also experiencing it. But I also believe that it is by no means necessary and essential to have those experiences in order to help someone really hurting from a tragic death. It may even interfere with the helping process, if the helping person, chaplain, or whoever, hasn't worked through his own feelings about death.

I say this simply because, as a family, we were helped by some who had not experienced anything like this, and by some who had. We were also turned off and further hurt by a few who may have meant well but apparently had so many hang-ups about death themselves that they tried to impose on us their easy answers and quick solutions to our deeply disturbing questions and our heavy, multifaceted problems (consisting of such things as shock, guilt, anger, regression, and confusion).

A simplistic sounding answer to the question of how to help families face tragedy is that, paradoxically, there are no "right things to say," nor is there even a need to say anything that speaks to the intellect at a time like this. The need is for sincere human love, reaching in its own unique, spontaneous, fumbling way with a "built-in" message: "Though I don't fully understand how you feel, I care enough to come to you and to try to share your hurt with you as much as I can, and as much as you will allow me to at this time. I'll leave you alone if I get any vibrations from you that you prefer to be alone, yet I'll leave with a readiness to come back when you give the signal you want me to come back." We were fortunate to have a lot of friends, colleagues, neighbors, and family members who did precisely this for us. Some examples might help.

Our young pastor first comes to mind. He came to our house early in the morning when he had heard the news of Tom's fatal accident, put his arms around us, and all he could say as his eyes began to moisten was, "Vern, I don't know what to say." This communicated a thousand times more than any words could what we needed at the time. Contrast that experience with the one we had with a pastor/colleague who came and with a radiant beam on his face announced, "How happy we can be to have a son in heaven!" My wife expressed a reaction to this as well: "What on earth did he want us to do? Have a celebration because our son was just killed?"

The hospital administrator came to our home with a generous supply of food later that day. He, too, was a person who had a way with words, but at that time his words were very awkward, though his feelings and actions were eloquent and beautiful. It wasn't until several months later that I learned he, too, had lost a child.

A word on the importance of the "caring communities." Expressions of care came to our four younger children from their school classmates and teachers. This helped them. Our daughter, exactly a year older than Tom, missed this at the more impersonal university she was attending. My wife was showered with attention and concern from her many friends where she worked. Our neighbors and many fellow church members reached out to us and continued to do so for quite some time. I mention this because of how it helped and how important it can be if we as chaplains and pastors and religious leaders can facilitate significant groups to express care to persons hurting from tragic deaths.

Time does indeed heal to some extent. Meanwhile, we continue to experience the truth of a Dietrich-Bonhoeffer inspired prayer statement that was incorporated by some of Lynn's classmates into a Memorial Mass offered for her:

"Nothing can fill the gap when we are away from those we love, and it would be wrong to try and find anything. We must simply hold out and win through. That sounds very hard at first, but at the same time it is a great consolation, since leaving the gap unfilled preserves the bond between us. It is nonsense to say that God fills the gap. He does not fill it, but keeps it empty so that our communion with another may be kept alive, even at the cost of pain."

Some may feel this irreverent and even blasphemous to say that God cannot (or does not) fill the void. I believe the opposite. No person you truly love can be replaced. If that were possible, something would be taken away from the special God-given uniqueness of that person and of the original relationship. We cannot help but think of a Christmas text from St. Paul: "When the fullness of time had come God sent forth His son . . . to redeem . . ." Redemptive love expressed with genuineness and with the special uniqueness of a person, be he or she a chaplain, pastor, volunteer, neighbor, or whoever, is what I believe most helps families face the pain of a tragic death.[2]

We must never presume to offer easy answers to painful, complex questions. We must allow room for anger, questions, probing, and the honest expression of pain in tragic situations. Shauna Larsen knows of that pain. Her husband, Joseph R. Larsen (whom she affectionately called "Jay"), died of cancer February 17, 1989. For most of their married life, he was confined to a wheelchair, and she was always at his side. I have met few people with greater faith but also with a greater capacity for openness. In the hope that her experience could help someone else, she shared the following:

> I have learned that it's okay to miss them, to talk to them, to be provoked with them, and, at the same time, to know that the Lord's hand was there. He wants us to know that we can make it and that we can take it! Elder Neal A. Maxwell's book *All These Things Shall Give Thee Experience*, helped me to understand that the Lord knows what we can take but we don't, and we have to find out! How can we be entrusted with eternal worlds of our own if we don't know we can make it here? How can we have empathy for those who are suffering if we have not experienced it ourselves? The Lord knows us better than we know us. He knows what I can do. I just have to find out for myself, to find

---

[2] Vern Albrecht. Reprinted by permission.

my own identity. For thirty-five years I never left Jay's side. Now the Lord is giving me a period of time to find out what I am all about. And when you begin to believe that your feelings are valid, you become a vocal advocate for yourself! Jay was half of my identity! Now I have to redefine myself. I have to decide what I can do and do it! Brent Barlow's book, *Understanding Death*, has been a great help. There is a line in the book that says "Self-mastery is making yourself do something you ought to do whether you want to or not."[3] Sometimes we don't reach for a book like that until our own desperate need leads us to it, but it helps to read about others who have gone through it!

How does it feel? You have a desire to stop taking care of yourself, to stop eating and sleeping. You don't feel like doing anything. You put a hold on your desires. You are angry! Anger is directed at the loss—at the one who died. Sometimes I say to Jay, "How dare you leave me like this?" It can be both funny and sad. It's okay to let all the anger out. You have to realize that you are who you are, and accept yourself as who you are. I cry easily, but that's me!

In the midst of our tears, it is important to have a sense of humor. You need to be able to laugh at yourself, at others, and at the one who is gone. I have a poem on my refrigerator that helps me laugh when I need to:

I like my bifocals—
My dentures fit me fine.
My hearing aid is perfect,
But, Lord, how I miss MY MIND!

The Lord tests us in ways we would least desire and least expect! He seems to give us the one challenge we feel sure we could not survive. A card from a friend said, "For all the knowledge we've gained we still can't make an overcast sky turn bright or keep the rain from falling. Sometimes we just have to walk through the storm." And you know, the Lord lets us! We have to know the cold, dark emptiness before we can know the light! It's like making a stew. You don't know what ingredients go into it until you make it yourself!

---

[3] Op. cit., *Understanding Death*, p. 77.

The Lord will give you peace. It does not come all at once. God expects us to work through the hurt. After we have done that, peace comes. Peace also comes through other people. The Lord sends them to help if you will listen. Find those people with whom you can talk and cry. Afterward, the "talk-tears" become fewer. Sometimes when we petition God for a miracle, or some glimpse of the loved one who died, it doesn't happen. I was asking for a sign that I don't need. I already know what I need to know!

We have to heal in a mortal way but also in a spiritual way. For us to see through God's eyes we must achieve a higher degree of spirituality that lets God's light shine within us! When I finally told the Lord, "I don't want Jay to suffer anymore. Thy will be done," he was gone in two days. Understanding death is for the living, not for those who died. Jay knows all about it. It's for us who are here to understand what death is and what life is. There are going to be more people on this earth who need this knowledge than ever before. We are living in a world where we will need preparation for the increasing turmoil ahead. Grief is a necessary work and a mortal task. We must learn to do it!

Through it all I have better learned how to help others. When you are going to see someone who is grieving, and you don't know what to say, share the relationship you had with that person, the funny, sweet feelings about them; the stories of what you had done together or about the difference he made in your life. Share what is special about the person who died. The most important message Jay gave to others in this life was, "Do the best you can with what you have. It's not your disability that counts. It's your ability." It was a comfort to me that, from a wheelchair, from actually living it himself, he inspired others to live it!

There were two posters in the oncology unit that really helped me. One said, "Life can only be understood backwards, but it must be lived forwards." (Soren Kierkegaard)

The other, by Hippocrates, said, "Healing is a matter of time, but it is also sometimes a matter of opportunity."

If you can only think of yourself, your grief turns inward. You have to turn it outward. Someday the hands we reach out to strengthen may be the same hands that reach back to strengthen us.

When Elder Todd Wilson was killed in Bolivia, his father, Arvil, said, "People would call us on the phone and say, 'We hate to bother you.' We were kept going constantly between the door and the telephone. But what if the phone never rang? How could we have gotten through this alone?"

His wife, Elaine, quickly added, "Hugs have meant so much to us. We are amazed at how much strength hugs have given us." She expressed her love and gratitude for the worldwide response and support that came to them at such a difficult time in their lives:

We are so grateful for the beautiful cards and words of comfort given to us from the moment we were told of Todd's death. We have been given so much love, food, financial assistance, and help in so many ways. Friends and family have come from all over to console us and be with us through this tragedy.

Our stake president and bishop have spent many hours of their time to help us, not only comforting us but cheering us up and taking care of many details that would have been very hard for us. A very talented and dear friend wrote and sang a song at the funeral titled, "Bless Our Todd Tonight." Our son-in-law and grandchildren also sang. Another dear friend sang one of our favorite hymns. Our son and daughter gave a tribute. The speeches and prayers were all a comfort. It was a very difficult time to speak or sing and they will be blessed.

The whole town brought food, not only to the house, but they also fed a whole cultural hall full of friends and relatives after the funeral.

Some of the cards came from as far away as Alaska, Florida, Argentina, and many other countries. Many of the cards and phone calls begin by saying, "You don't know me, but we have been praying and shedding many tears for you." Several of them had had tragedies in their own lives and had many words of comfort for us. Many had missionaries and

expressed their grief. Some had even met Todd and had seen
him since we have and loved him almost as much as we do.
One of Todd's converts wrote to us and said, "Todd died that
I might live."

We have had calls of condolences and love from many of
our General Authorities and Church leaders. They have
helped give us much peace of mind. Their prayers have been
in our behalf many times.

We had many offers of homes and trailers to put up our
many relatives from out of town. We had friends come in and
clean our house and take care of the food brought to us. But
most of all, we have had love and friendship and comfort,
both physical and spiritual. We want to thank all those who
responded to us in such sensitive and meaningful ways.

At a Canadian workshop, a woman came bringing a
beautiful quilt and some teddy bears. When her beloved
husband died she puzzled about what to do with his clothes,
especially his shirts. The arms of the shirts had held her so
many times! She decided to cut the clothes up and make
quilting squares. Many friends came to work on the quilt
and write in a memory book. She now tucks her small
daughter in at night in the quilt made of her daddy's shirts.

When her neighbor's wife died she made teddy bears of her
lovely dresses. She put his wife's favorite perfume in the stuffing
that went into the bears, so two small boys would be able to
keep, for awhile, the fragrance of their mother next to them.

I am always touched by the creative ways people find to
help and comfort each other!

It is a very special privilege to witness help and healing
during a time of crisis. In my work I have been reminded
many times of the trust placed in friends and in church
leaders when the need is greatest. A little boy whose father
had just committed suicide expressed this trust in a note he
wrote in his children's support group. "The advice I would
give to a person whose parent dies is just be calm. Then act

normal, and then call your bishop. He will come over and calm you down some more. And then it's over."

The trust of those who grieve is a sacred trust, and we must respond with the best that is in us. It requires much prayer, study, and humility to respond to this great mission of comforting. It would be helpful if church leaders could have a workable plan in the event of catastrophic disability or death. At the time the loss occurs, the family may need help to notify other family members about the death. Family members need to know it is okay to be assertive and state their needs. If they need time alone with the person who died, that opportunity should be extended. The family needs the freedom to conduct the funeral service their way, with minimal interference. The funeral service facilitates closure for survivors and symbolizes the person who died. There may be special songs or tributes, and their inclusion in the service may be of vital importance to family members. This is a time for families to express grief in a creative way. They have no control over the death. The last vestige of control for the family is the planning of the funeral or memorial service. Families should be given as much agency as possible for this time of mortal good-byes.

It may be helpful to have a meeting of all church leaders immediately after a funeral. For example, if a death occurs in a family of six children of varied ages, the bishop, the Sunday School president, the elders quorum president, the Young Men and Young Women presidents, and the Relief Society president could assist in the planning of a coordinated effort to help. Home teachers and visiting teachers could also be included in this meeting. Sunday school teachers could be contacted to talk with children in their classes about the loss, and perhaps a child from the bereaved family could share feelings with the class. So that one person is not responsible for everyone, each leader could plan to support the child in the age group with which they work.

The elders quorum could assist with needed yard work and other difficult tasks in the home. Letters and pictures from children are a comfort to younger as well as older family members. The Wilson family was touched by some big red paper hearts that Primary children had written messages on. Relief Society sisters could attend to housework, laundry, and meals.

Dick Obershaw suggests that when food is brought to a grieving family, it should not be brought in a disposable dish or an old casserole dish that has been used for twenty years and has someone's name on the bottom. Food should be brought in the most beautiful dish you have. Fill it up with your favorite food, take it to the family, and say, "This is my dish. I'll come back for it." From experience I have learned that those who are grieving may find it very hard to return stacks of dishes. Unless a name is on a dish they may not remember who it belongs to. Some stay on the cupboard for weeks, and sometimes a child or neighbor is enlisted to return the dish. It works better to go back to the house to get the dish and, while there, to find out if the person who is grieving would like to talk about the loss.

"Would you like to talk about it?" is always an appropriate question. If they want to talk at that particular time they will. If not, at least a door has been opened that they can walk through later. The Relief Society could make sure that Mom gets out of the house now and then and has some time for herself to go for a walk, to a good movie, or to simply go window shopping. Personal letters from bishoprics and other auxiliaries are always deeply appreciated. Family members should be asked if they would like a special priesthood blessing.

Follow-up contact could be made periodically for several months following the loss. Families should be encouraged to remember their loved ones. When holidays come, special ideas could be given to include the person who died during the holidays. For example, at Christmas time a stocking, with the name of the person who died on it, could be filled with special notes and gifts and shared in a family home evening. Since a divorce is like a death, similar help and support could be given to a family who has experienced this loss. The needs of a family going through a divorce are great. Food and flowers would be more helpful than judgmental statements or prying questions.

I was moved by a poem that eloquently expresses the need we all have to be of service to others who are hurting.

To My Friend in Your Grief

It seems so useless to say,
Is there anything I can do for you?
I know what I can do.
If you want company,
I will stay with you.
If you want to talk,
I will listen;
If you want to listen,
I will talk.
If you want to eat,
I will serve you;
If you refuse to eat,
I will understand.
Yes, my friend, there is something I can do for you.
I can share your hurt
And maybe make it easier to bear.
Most of all, I will lift your name in prayer,
Seeking your comfort.
I will help you carry your sorrow to the feet of Jesus,
Who has promised "peace that passeth understanding."
Dear friend, I LOVE YOU! [3]

I have learned an important truth about the principle of service. It has two important aspects:

1. We must be willing to give ourselves away to others.

2. We must be willing to allow others to give themselves to us!

---

[3] Simmons, Kay, *Home Life*, Mar. 1986, p. 16.

A dear friend of mine in Colorado took her own life. She was talented and sensitive and had so much to give. Determined to find a reason why she took her life, I read over all the letters she had sent to me. One of the letters contained a clue I had missed. She wrote, "In your state of Utah you have a body of water called the Great Salt Lake. One of the reasons it is salty is because water can flow into it but not out of it. It is like the Dead Sea, and *I* am like the Dead Sea."

Love is a process of both giving and receiving, and somewhere along the way, Linda had lost her capacity to give or to recieve. When our capacity to give or to receive love is blocked, the quality of our lives is damaged. There are times when it is more important for us to give and times when it is more important to receive.

A few years ago I received a letter from Roger Chapman in Washington.

> Deanna, you don't know me, but several nights ago I went to sleep with my radio on and woke up at about 2:00 A.M. to your beautiful voice and words which brought me wide awake. I have not rested until I finally found a way to obtain a copy of those words. I heard it over a Sacred Heart radio program out of St. Louis, but I caught only your name and the general words of the song, anticipating I would just go downtown and pick up a copy. No one had heard of it. I finally traced the station in St. Louis, and the manager of the station gave me your address. I caught only the last of the song which says something about not being able to live until you give yourself away. I am in need of help in obtaining your tape.

He was referring to the song, "Give Yourself Away."

> The gift of you is priceless! I'm glad to be your friend.
> No one like you has ever been or will ever be again.
> The love you give so gladly is in my heart to stay.
> You're heaven-made, don't be afraid to give yourself away.
> Tomorrow lies within you, glowing like a flame.
> The hope of generations is written in your name,

The light that shines within you will turn the night to day.
You're heaven-made, don't be afraid to give yourself away!

Roger had been through some painful experiences in his own life and recognized that the road to healing would come with the courage to give himself away. He became involved with a group of Hospice Volunteers and wrote this beautiful letter, "To A Dying Friend:"

Hello, my friend,

I am here to walk through the shadows and into the sunlight with you. Many years ago a special event occurred in your life that was very beautiful and tender. What took place was your birth. When you were born there were so many people awaiting your arrival, and there was nothing more important on their minds at that time, nor were they engaged in any activity that kept them from being as close as possible to where you were born.

Plans had been made and completed in anticipation of that great day. Your mother had lovingly scrubbed and cleaned your room and decorated it with soft things, pictures, and loving words framed in delicate colors. Tiny clothes filled the dresser, and rattles and toys lay waiting on the shelf just for you. When you decided it was time, you came, and within minutes you were snuggled in your mother's arms. She held you so close you could feel her heart beating and feel her soft kisses upon your pink, wrinkled face. Those loving arms and hands held and nurtured you through those days when all you could do was just lay there and let it happen. It was so gentle and comfortable just letting it be.

So, now, when your arms are too weak to hold your babies anymore, and you can't scrub the floors and cook the meals, and you know that your health is failing and you wonder about tomorrow, let me walk with you awhile, hold your hand, and we will step into tomorrow together.

When you came into this world, you were surrounded by love and kindness, and you were held and cherished, and you were the most important person all around the neighborhood. You had to be taken care of, and your family and friends did it with hearts bursting with joy and pride. When you brought your children into the world, there was nothing more important than serving your baby and taking care of his every need. Your heart was full and warm.

Now the circle is complete. Will you let those people whom you lovingly held in your arms and nurtured now be to you what you were to them? And if they can't always be here, will you let me, a new friend, take up those tasks for you? Will you let my hands become your hands, and my feet your feet? The circle is complete as it should be. You are the most important person right now. Loving hands wait to minister to you; eyes gaze affectionately upon you; arms encircle you and lift you up; they hold you. It is time once again to just let it be; let love wrap you up and take care of you. I will be with you as you die in love's arms. Perhaps in so doing I will learn how to live! Thank you for that gift!

Your friend, Roger

Roger himself died recently, in the loving presence of his family and friends. So many people were grateful for his service to his community through hospice. The final years of his life were made richer because of his unfailing service to others.

The following is a letter that taught me in an unforgettable way the importance of allowing those who are lacking in physical capacity to give of their special gifts to us.

Dear Deanna,

You have been on my mind and in my heart since you appeared in Marshfield, Wisconsin, for Wood County Social Services. I talked with you for a brief moment after the program and shared with you my struggle with cancer and felt your deep concern for me. I want to thank you for that concern and support but something occurred to me at that moment and has been on my mind since.

Sometimes people like myself with life-threatening illnesses are so willing to take and to receive. Granted, our needs are great, and I know that you understand that. But why didn't I ask you how you were, what bugs you, what makes you feel happy or sad, and express my deep interest in you as a person and in the continuation of your career and mission? I have had the opportunity to listen and share with you twice. On the first occasion I was a closet cancer patient, not talking, keeping everything locked up inside. Consequently, a large ulcer formed in my stomach.

Then I met you and you helped me to understand something. It is this: dying from cancer is not very hard to do, but living with it can be the real culprit. Distress both physical and emotional is abundant, and not much is known or done about emotional distress. But part of loving is giving and part is receiving, and until you experience both, you can never live or love to the utmost!

At this point in time I am more concerned about spiritual health than I am the physical, and by the way, the physical seems to be taking care of itself; my remission continues and my ulcer is healed. I have humbled myself and asked for help and received so much more than I knew even existed from family, friends, and yes, sometimes even passing acquaintances.

I feel strong again in a new way. I guess I've looked death in the face and found it not to be so sinister. Thank you for writing the song, "Teach Me To Die." The song is right, you know. Now I can live more fully and even extend my hand to love and support others! You know, Deanna, you are either alive or dead. The transition is very short and I, for one, will not be absolved of my responsibilities to my fellow brothers and sisters. Wouldn't it be nice the day I die to be able to do something for someone else? I am asking you to expect this from me and settle for nothing less. It will make me and all others faced with life-threatening illnesses or disabilities better persons. It will extend our lives and bring us so much closer to Almighty God.

So, I am asking you, Deanna, how is life going? What are your hopes, your fears, what makes you laugh and cry? What is your favorite color? (I know you love donuts and yellow roses!) I express my sincere concern that all is well with you and your God. Peace, Deanna, peace. You are never alone. I have carved you on the palm of my hand.

> Fondly,
> Charlotte Quick
> Wisconsin Rapids, Wisconsin

Throughout the world, volunteers and hospice groups in private homes, hospitals, and nursing homes render quiet, life-giving service. I have long admired the work of Mother Teresa of Calcutta, India. A wiry, energetic woman, she carries the hope of the world in her weathered face and all that she owns in a small bag. The winner of the Nobel Peace Prize in 1979 for her work with the sick and dying in the poverty-stricken streets of Calcutta, she sees the face of Christ in all the people she touches. She is well loved among the peoples in India and throughout the world. She teaches us by example, as well as with words, that each of us can be involved in the important work of comforting the sick and making the world a more loving place. From her I have learned some very valuable lessons about service. Malcolm Muggeridge expresses well the philosophy she lives by.

No one must drift away from the humble works, because these are the works nobody will do. It is never too small. We are so small we look at things in a small way. But God, being Almighty, sees everything great. Therefore, even if you write a letter for a blind man, or you just go and sit and listen, or you take the mail for them, or you visit somebody or bring a flower to somebody—small things—or wash clothes for somebody or clean the house . . . Very humble work, that is where you and I must be. For there are many people who can do the big things. We can do very little for the people, but at least they know that we love them, that we care for them and that we are anxious to help them. Let us try, all of us, to come closer to that unity of spreading Christ's love wherever we go. Love and compassion. Have deep compassion for the people. People are suffering much, very much: mentally, physically, in every possible way. So you are the ones to bring that hope, that love, that kindness. Do you want to do something beautiful for God? There is a person who needs you. This is your chance.[4]

---

[4] Muggeridge, Malcolm, *Something Beautiful for God: Mother Teresa of Calcutta.*

There are five principles of service we can apply when we want to help those who are hurting.

1. *Know thyself.* Come to know and understand your own fears and feelings about death, pain, and illness before you try to help someone else.

2. *Listen with a sense of leisure.* Always listen with your heart, with relaxed body position, with eye-to-eye contact. Avoid glancing at your wristwatch, and if you have a time limit, let the person know that the specific time you do have is all theirs.

3. *Don't be afraid to touch.* Hugs are for healing. Many people who were grieving have told me how comforting it was simply to be held, a language so powerful that no words were necessary. Those who may be uncomfortable with hugging may welcome the touch of a hand or just the physical presence of someone who cares. Just as the touch of the Master's hand on an old violin can create beautiful music, the Savior's touch can be felt when we welcome others into the open arms of our love.

4. *Follow up.* After death, divorce, accident, injury, or illness, let that person know weeks and months later that you love them and have not forgotten them. I remember going one day to see a friend whose husband had died the year before. When she saw me on her porch with my guitar she exclaimed, "My husband died a year ago today. How did you know I needed you?" We sat in her kitchen, sang his favorite songs, and talked about their memories. "When we were first married," she said, "I made a batch of jelly that was so hard Frank could stick a knife into the jar, hold it upside down, and none of the jelly would run out!" How special it was to get to know him through her memories!

5. *Communicate openly and honestly.* This is one of the most important principles because words have the power to heal or to hurt after a loss has occurred. Grief leaves us feeling isolated as if no one in the world has ever felt the pain we are

feeling now, as if no one knows what we know. Perhaps one of the most difficult challenges is to master the art of what to say when someone is grieving. Words are such fragile things, and yet they have such power! Words thoughtlessly spoken can wound deeply. Because we are so vulnerable when we grieve, we seem to remember such words clearly. Years later, people are able to recall almost the exact words that were spoken and who said them. By the same token, people remember the words or the thought that broke through the clouds of their grief and, for a brief moment, brought them the warm bright rays of the sun. They remember the kindness and the empathy that gave them a reason to smile again.

It would be easy to resign ourselves to tranquil ignorance and be silent. We are all experts when it comes to our own grief, but we cannot comprehend fully the pain of another. The path of least resistance may be silence when we are in doubt. Fearful of the impact of words we speak, we could avoid those who are dying and those who are grieving so we will risk no verbal confrontations. But to risk is to live!

"The person who risks nothing, does nothing, has nothing, and is nothing, and though he may avoid suffering and sorrow, he simply cannot learn, feel, change, grow, love, or live. Chained by his certitudes he has become a slave and has forfeited freedom. Only the person who risks is truly free!"

Author Unknown

So, if we make the decision to risk and break the fragile silence that stands between us, knowing that we can shatter a heart as well as mend it, it would be well for us to learn how to communicate with an open heart. We will become more gentle with others because we have made the same mistakes ourselves in the past. We will become tolerant because insensitivity and fear are close companions. We will become more forgiving when we realize others do not *intend* to hurt us when they say or do insensetive things.

I have discovered that the best way to learn how to develop appropriate communication skills is to avoid judgments. When others label subjects such as death and grief as being "morbid" or "depressing," I look upon those comments as disguised fear. If a dying patient believes that his dying process is morbid to you, he will not allow bonds to be formed that could teach you how to live and love. I have learned much about communication by asking my audiences two questions:

1. *Do you remember anything said or done during a time you were grieving that hurt you?*

2. *Do you remember anything said or done during a time of loss that helped you?*

Those who grieve will tell us what hurts and what helps, and as the years go by we will develop an intrinsic sensitivity that will help us to help others. I have countless pages in my files of comments that hurt and those that help. It would take a book just to record them all. Unfortunately, I have more lists of insensitive statements that people have made than I have sensitive ones, which points out the extent of our failure to communicate effectively. For example, I recently met the mother of a little child with Down's Syndrome. She told me that an unthinking friend had said to her, "I would rather have my child be born dead than to have a child born with mental or physical disabilities." This comment brought this young mother so much pain when it was spoken that even now it is very traumatic for her to recall.

For the sake of brevity, I will share only a few of the most commonly mentioned hurtful comments, and some of the helpful ones. Each person who reads this will be able to think of many more as they reflect on their own experiences. It is important to remember that what helps one person may hurt another. The phrase "I'm sorry" is an example. It is a delicate phrase because it can be misinterpreted so easily. If

it is a statement of empathy, it can be helpful. If it is interpreted to mean "I feel sorry for you," the person making the
statement has just placed himself in a position of superiority.
Pity is rarely welcomed by those who grieve; empathy is.
Here are some examples of hurtful comments.

"IT'S GOD'S WILL."

I have never met anyone who was comforted by this statement. Orville Kelly, a cancer patient from Iowa, said he got
tired of people telling him that his cancer was God's will. One
day a sensitive friend said, "Kelly, I think that cancer is God's
enemy, and I think He's hurting with you." Kelly said the
statement brought more comfort to him than he could
express. It brought comfort to me as well several years later. I
was on my way to San Francisco to conduct a seminar when I
read in the paper that some friends living in that area had
been shot to death in their home. During that traumatic time
someone said to me, "It must have been God's will. He has a
time for all of us to die." I quickly replied, "No, I think that
murder is God's enemy, and I think He's hurting with me."

"I UNDERSTAND EXACTLY HOW YOU FEEL."

Our pain is unique to us. No one in the world can have any
idea what we are feeling or define for us the impact of our
losses. However, it is easier for parents who have lost a child to
relate to other parents who have experienced the same loss.
That is why support groups are so valuable during times of
grief. It is helpful to communicate with others who have gone
through losses that are similar to ours, but the phrase "I know
just what you are going through" is one we should always avoid.

"SOMETHING A LOT WORSE THAN THAT HAPPENED TO ME!"

Bonnie Bright wrote, "I realize today more than ever that
comparing pain and loss does not help. There will always be

someone whose horror was greater, suffering more prolonged, death more tragic, or situation more devastating. But when you take away the horror, the quantity of time, the tragedy of 'how,' you have the very same result—a hole, an emptiness in the life or lives of the survivors. Comparing the devastation only makes you belittle your ability to cope. If we insist on comparing notes, maybe we should compare ways to bridge the emptiness or fill the hole. By doing this, we might avoid the anguish that can develop by comparing, collecting, and counting losses instead of sharing, giving, and being seeds of blessings."

"DON'T CRY. YOU'LL SEE HIM AGAIN."

The first part of this statement suggests that if you have enough faith in immortality, mortal tears are not necessary, and that tears may even suggest a lack of faith. Referring to the second part of the statement, a woman said, "It was like being told I could have a drink of water in thirty years when I am dying of thirst on a desert now." Emotional freedom is essential to healing, and the long, arduous journey through mortality can seem quite empty without the company and companionship of a beloved family member or friend. When we lose a loved one we mourn the loss of that gentle touch, a knowing smile, someone to get the lawn mower started, the fragrant smells from the kitchen, and the heart-felt embrace. We mourn not only the loss of someone we loved but of someone who loved us in a special way we may not be loved again. To give that loneliness a voice, I wrote the following song,

I Lost the One Who Loved Me Yesterday

You can't know how it feels until you've been there,
When one last good-bye is all that you can say.
I won't wake up to kiss him every morning,
'Cause I lost the one who loved me yesterday.

We lived together forty years next August
On a little farm beneath Nebraska skies.
Together from the earth we made our living,

And the bright sun rose and set in Bobby's eyes.

It's hard to put one setting on the table.
I'd give anything to hold him just once more.
God help me through the times when I remember
That my Bobby won't be coming through that door!

I need so much your helping hand to guide me.
Without your love I may not find the way.
Remember I'll still need you next September,
'Cause I lost the one who loved me yesterday.

"HE LIVED A LONG LIFE. HE WAS READY TO GO."

This is called "minimizing grief." Sometimes we minimize grief in terms of age. Some believe that if the person
who died was very old or very young we don't have to grieve
as much for them. At her beloved grandfather's funeral, a
friend of mine heard someone say, "He lived a long life. He
was ready to go!" One woman, whose baby died at birth,
was actually told, "You should be glad your baby died before
you learned to love her." Years later, that statement
continues to be an ache in her heart. Equally painful is the
advice to "Hurry and have another baby to take the place of
the one you lost" or "Why are you grieving so much for the
child who died? You still have seven other children!" When a
handicapped child dies a parent is sometimes told, "It was
for the best." Quite often, when a woman has a miscarriage,
she is told, "It was for the best." When a loss is not acknowl-
edged it is called "disenfrachised grief." Many people are
living with losses that go unrecognized by the families and
the society in which they live. There are many rooms in the
human heart, just as there are many rooms in the heart of
God. Each loved one occupies a room in your heart that will
never be filled by anyone else. Whether Grandpa is eighty-
five or a baby is a day old, the pain of loss is just as real. We
should be able to respect the pain of someone's loss without
feeling a need to minimize it.

"AREN'T YOU OVER THE DEATH OF YOUR LOVED ONE YET?"

A woman whose three-year-old son died in a farm accident was asked six months later, "Aren't you over his death yet?" I have often pondered on the meaning of the words, "getting over." Perhaps, to many, it means to "forget." "Haven't you forgotten your son's death yet?" is the way the mother heard the question. My friend Faye, whose husband died, began to hear the question, "When are you going to forget him and start living again?" She answered with this eloquent poem:

> You ask me to forget him, say I'm living in the past,
> That memories are useless, no love could ever last.
> I want to live without him and I want to love once more,
> But don't ask me to forget him or completely close that door.
> We lived so long together. We shared our hopes and dreams.
> Those memories are important and they mean a lot to me.
> Why can't you understand those years can't be erased?
> He died, but once he lived, a part of this human race,
> And if I forget him completely it's like he never lived!

"GOD GAVE YOU THIS TRIAL TO MAKE YOU STRONGER."

Most people would say, "I'd rather be weaker right now, thank you." A wonderful book for everyone to read is *When Bad Things Happen to Good People*, by Rabbi Harold Kushner. He explains that God did not cause all of our problems and heartaches, nor does He reward us for righteous living with constant protection. He does allow us to live in a world governed by agency, illness, and natural disaster. Even when we are doing our best, tragedy can come to us as quickly as it can come to anyone else. It is not helpful at the time of a tragic loss to hear someone say, "Look how much you are going to grow from this experience." It is true that, as we look back after a loss, we can see areas of personal growth, but at the time of loss it is not a helpful reminder. It can sound as if someone is saying that growth is a suitable substitute for the absence of a loved one.

"IF YOU HAVE ENOUGH FAITH, YOU WILL GET WELL."

Our neighbors had a lovely daughter who was dying of cancer. One day a well-meaning friend called and said, "Tell Kathy that if she has enough faith she will get well." Kathy died shortly afterward. Her mother called me one day, close to tears, and said, "Please tell people not to say this to families who have a loved one who is dying. I don't know of anyone who had a greater faith than Kathy's."

"SHE IS MUCH BETTER OFF IN HEAVEN. SHE WILL BE HAPPIER THERE."

For parents who have lovingly prepared a beautiful nursery for a new baby or to someone who has been caring for a terminally ill loved one, this statement may be offensive. The comment, "Now you won't be so tied down," never helps. One man remembers someone saying to him when he was small, "Your dad will be of more help to you from the 'other side' than he would have been here." He said, "My mom had so many struggles, and we missed Dad so much that I never believed that statement." *It is important when we communicate that we do not try to read the mind of God and interpret it for someone else.*

"BECAUSE YOUR CHILD TOOK HIS OWN LIFE, YOU WILL NEVER BE TOGETHER IN THE ETERNITIES."

God has a great heart! Only He knows of the conditions and circumstances that cause people to take their own lives. There are times when we cannot give another person the will to live, when, as one mother said, "love is not enough." The causes of suicide are numerous, and we are only just beginning to identify some of them: chemical imbalance, emotional instability, severe trauma, mental illness, and extreme dependence, as well as pressure and expectations of peers and society. To be nonjudgmental is the most important attribute we can have when we are trying to help a family who has experienced this tragic loss. I was moved by a statement made at the funeral of a young man who took his own life. The speaker said, "He was like the owner of a car that ran out of gas and he just didn't know how to fill it back up!"

For other sensitive problems, the most commonly mentioned "not helpful" comments are:

"AREN'T YOU MARRIED YET?"

This is a painful question to those who would like to marry but have not had the opportunity, to those who have gone through a divorce, or to those who have chosen to remain single for reasons they may not want to share with others. Telling someone whose spouse has died to "hurry and start dating again" is also inappropriate. Those who are single because of death, divorce, lack of opportunity, or choice are already painfully aware that we live in a society where the emphasis is on "families." We can better help make those adjustments by sharing loving and accepting attitudes.

"WHAT DO YOU DO WITH YOUR CHILDREN WHEN YOU'RE AT WORK?"

Women who find it necessary to work outside the home miss their children deeply and often grieve because they are not able to "be there" when a child comes home from school. To a single parent or to one whose financial needs make working a necessity, this question can add to an already heavy burden. A working mother may not wish to share her reasons for working or the arrangements for care that she has made for her children with a casual acquaintance. It is a personal matter between her, her family, and her Father in Heaven.

"WHOSE FAULT WAS THE DIVORCE, YOURS OR YOUR HUSBAND'S?"

While this thought may not be verbalized, many people are thinking it. This is evidenced by the fact that when death occurs, the family is usually surrounded by loving friends, food, and flowers. When divorce happens an emotional death has occurred, but it is not recognized as such by church and community. It is another form of grief that is often disenfranchised. Perhaps the friend who is going through a divorce could use a bouquet of flowers and a simple note which says, "I care." Mentors from church and community could spend extra time with children who are suddenly left without a parent.

What Helps?

Often, it is not what we say that people remember. In retrospect, they may remember only your presence or the way they felt when you hugged them. When we allow ourselves to walk with someone through their suffering, we soon learn that what we say is not as important as how we feel inside. If we can discard our own fears and relate to those who grieve, important lessons about loving and living can be learned. Soon communication will become natural, and we will speak with our hearts. The following comments have been helpful to those who were hurting.

"I LOVE YOU."

I have never met anyone who was too old, too hurt, or too tired to be loved. I have never known the words "I love you" to be offensive. When we are hurting, it helps to feel needed and wanted. Love affirms another person's right to be and to feel what he feels. To love is to be nonjudgmental and ever present. Love breaks up the terrible anonymity of loneliness. Thomas Wolf said, "Love is the ultimate expression of the will to live."

"YOU'RE NOT ALONE. I AM WITH YOU."

It is a source of comfort to know that through the adversities we face, we will not be alone. No one should have to die alone and no one should have to live alone. Knowing that a friend will tend or bind up our wounds with a gentle and tender hand, and laugh with us when we want to celebrate life again, is a comfort. A woman whose husband died told me that this poem helped her to feel his comfort and encouragement and to remember that she would never be alone.

> If I should die and leave you here awhile,
> Be not like others, sore undone,
> Who keep long vigil by the silent dust and weep.
> For my sake turn again to life and smile,
> Nerving thy heart and trembling hand
> To do something to comfort weaker souls than thine.
> Complete there, dear, unfinished tasks of mine
> And I, perchance, may therein comfort you.
> (Author Unknown)

"I REMEMBER WHEN . . ."

What a joy it is for a grieving person to have someone else tell them about a special memory they shared with a loved one who died. It can be about an event or quality that was observed in their loved one. Saying, "She made a difference in my life because . . ." in a written memory can be reread in the future. Scrapbooks with pictures, quotations we remember that person saying, or humorous events are also deeply appreciated. Many people have told me how great it is to hear their loved one's name spoken in spontaneous expression, whether it is immediately following the loss or many months later. Names are precious and should never be forgotten. A little boy was hit by a car and died of sustained injuries. His mother became hurt and frustrated because, as time went by, no one mentioned her son's name. "I wondered," she said, "had everyone forgotten him so soon? One day a man came up to me and said, 'I remember when Johnny was our paperboy. We used to have him come in for hot chocolate and cookies when it was cold out. We really grew to love him, and we want you to know that we miss him and that we will not forget him.'" She continued, "He gave me more with that memory than he could have given me with a bushel of gold!"

"WHAT ARE YOUR NEEDS RIGHT NOW?"

This is a gentle, probing question that should be asked in an atmosphere of intimacy, preferably in person rather than over the telephone. This will give them the opportunity to express urgent personal needs in a climate of trust.

Be there.

Many people have told me that just having someone come and quietly share their presence helped a great deal. One day our neighbor's son was killed in a car accident. Our son baked some cookies and went to their home and quietly sat for a time, just "being" with them. Later, our friends told us what a comfort it was to know that our son, Shon wanted to be with them when they were faced with the most difficult experience of their lives. All of us feel helpless and impotent in the face of grief. None of us knows precisely what to say or do. If we can just take ourselves to the doorstep and say, "I am here," that is enough.

Share some special music.

Music is a wonderful way to communicate with someone who is grieving. I have found it to be the single most important tool in my work. I was in New Zealand in an acute care trauma unit in a hospital in Wellington. A beautiful young woman had been molested, beaten, and left in a park to die. She was from India and had come to New Zealand to work. She had been there only two weeks when the attack occurred. She had sustained severe brain injuries, and they did not think she could hear us. When I sang a song to her in her native language, we noticed coordinated eye movements, and tears slipped down her cheeks. We believe that she heard us. In my work with patients, as well as in grief counseling, music that conveys our feelings can be a great help in healing a broken heart.

Jana Miller wrote a beautiful thank-you in a recent news editorial in the *Lincoln Journal* in Lincoln, Nebraska. It was written in honor of her friend, Mary Obrist, a week following her death. She expresses thanks on behalf of Mary's family. Her editorial gives us valuable suggestions on how to help others during a time of catastrophic illness.

Jerry Obrist asked me to tell all of you thank you. "Thank you for the food you cooked. Thank you for the hours you cared for the children. Thank you for cleaning floors and folding laundry, for picking up last-minute items at the grocery store, for calling just to say hello, for keeping the Obrist family together during the last sorrow-filled year.

"All the help we have had . . . has gotten us through this last year, for which we will be forever grateful," Jerry told me last Saturday, just hours after his wife, Mary, forty, died peacefully at her home.

There's little room for thank-you's in newspapers' traditional obituary columns and news stories, measured in precious inches. But I see no better opportunity than this editorial page to thank the hundreds of family members and friends who unselfishly gave of their time and kindness to help others in need.

And so, on behalf of Mary and Jerry, I am taking this opportunity to offer thanks. I know Mary would approve, for she and I talked about just such a gesture several times.

I have come to understand that when tragedy strikes, the human spirit responds with generosity and creativity that no one knew existed. So it was in Mary's life. From the moment she was diagnosed with inflammatory breast cancer last

August, friends, family members, neighbors, former students, professional colleagues, mothers of her children's friends, and church people everywhere responded tirelessly.

There were teachers and secretaries, priests and parishioners, quilters and collectors, and good people who brought Mary comfort through prayer. More than one hundred people responded when asked to record memories of their times with Mary in a book given to her on her 40th birthday in February.

Cards and letters sent to cheer her and to let her know she was being remembered fill a bushel basket, Jerry says. Small quilt squares with appliqued hearts poured in from women who shared her love of quilting, some by women Mary had never met. Other quilters stitched their hearts into a quilt Mary had pieced earlier for her oldest daughter, Gretchen, eleven. And still other women opened their homes to Mary's younger daughters, Laura, four, and Karen, one.

"The community outpouring of love and time and dedication has been just incredible," said Barb Morton, director of the Lincoln Center who counseled Mary during her illness. "The hours spent, the sharing of time, which is the most valuable thing any of us have, has been amazing. It speaks so highly of Mary."

Barb says it is admirable that so many people have been so willing to help, putting themselves in the difficult situation of walking into a young mother's home, knowing that it was unlikely she would live long, and watching her grow weaker.

"Everybody's piece has mattered. And so for all of you who gave Mary just a small piece of comfort, thank you. Your willingness," says Barb, "says something incredibly special about human nature."[1]

Steven L. Channing's lovely thirteen-year-old daughter committed suicide, after he and his wife went through a painful divorce. He sought help from the support group, Compassionate Friends, and wrote a poem that would be a promise to help and support others.

---

[1] Reprinted by permission: Lincoln Journal, Licoln, Nebraska.

Your Compassionate Friend
In loving memory of my precious daughter, Kimberly

I can tell by that look, friend, that you need to talk,
So come take my hand and let's go for a walk.
See, I'm not like the others. I won't shy away,
Because I want to hear what you've got to say.

Your child has died and you need to be heard,
But they don't want to hear a single word.
They tell you your child's "with God, so be strong."
They say all the "right" things that somehow seem wrong.

They're just hurting for you and trying to say,
They'd give anything to help take your pain away.
But they're struggling with feelings they can't understand
So forgive them for not offering a helping hand.

I'll walk in your shoes for more than a mile.
I'll wait while you cry and be glad if you smile.
I won't criticize you or judge you or scorn.
I'll just stay and listen 'til your night turns to morn.

Yes, the journey is hard and unbearably long,
And I know you think that you're not quite that strong,
So just take my hand 'cause I've got time to spare,
And I know how it hurts, friend, for I have been there.

See, I owe a debt you can help me repay
For not long ago, I was helped the same way.
And I stumbled and fell through a world so unreal
So believe when I say that I sense how you feel.

I don't look for praise or for financial gain,
And I'm sure not the kind who gets joy out of pain.
I'm just a strong shoulder who'll be here 'til the end—
I'll promise to be your compassionate friend.

Henry Nowen said:

The Friend who can stay with us in an hour of grief and bereavement, who can tolerate not knowing, not healing, not curing, and face with us the reality of our powerlessness; that is the friend who cares!

Those who work closely with the grieving in counseling, in support groups, or in common friendships learn that even in the process of healing some good-byes are necessary. As a flower pushes upward toward the sun, so the person who is growing away from grief may gradually grow away from you. This does not mean they stop loving you or remembering the special bonds you shared during a time of acute loss, but the breaking away is sometimes very difficult for the person who helped the grieving family because they began to feel "so necessary."

It has been said that the greatest teacher is the one who renders himself unnecessary. When someone cries in your arms, when you walk with them through pain, you are allowed a rare glimpse into their hearts. No one can stay that vulnerable all the time, and the rain of tears eventually gives way to sunshine. Growth is a sign of healing. As time goes by and those extraordinary needs are filled with the reinvestment in life of the grieving person, the care giver may assume a less vital role. Just remember, you were an important part of a painful chapter in their lives. There will always be love and bonds of trust because of that. It was a chapter you all wrote together and through the experience you grew closer. Now the family must go on to write new chapters in their lives. It is okay for them to reread the chapters of the past now and then, but we must allow growth to take us in new directions, even when those directions take us away from each other.

Kathy Bradford of Brigham City, Utah, wrote a moving letter that reminded me of the importance of simply "being there."

Dear Deanna,

A couple of weeks ago I became discouraged after a day of visiting some of the needy sisters in my church. I felt such empathy for them, particularly for two young mothers whose husbands are battling cancer, but my tears and concern for them seemed so futile. I wondered to myself what possible difference do I make to these people? I haven't changed a thing for them or eased their suffering in any way.

I offered a silent prayer, asking that I might become more effective, and then a strange thing happened. Instead of going home as planned, I found myself driving up to the local bookstore and almost involuntarily going inside. There I found your tape. When I opened it, the folder inside fell open to the words of your song, "That's Enough." I felt as though it had been written just for me, and it changed my approach to my calling. I'm doing almost exactly the same things as before, but now instead of trying to change other's circumstances, I'm working to increase the quality of my love. That has made all the difference. Thank you so much for this song.

Love,
Kathy Bradford

I recieved the inspiration to write the song by the beautiful words of Sam Keene:

Intimacy is both terrifying and wonderful because it shatters our safe boundaries and polished self-images. When we touch, and allow ourselves to be touched, we are enlarged and changed by the contact. True intimacy comes only after we discover, after a thousand failures, that we can never take away each other's loneliness, fill the void in the bottom of the heart, make the world safe, banish tragedy, or take away the shadow of death. In the end, the best we can do is hold each other in this luminous darkness. And if, through our struggles, we finally come to be close to each other, that is enough!"[5]

"That's Enough" is a healing song because it reminds me, though I cannot take away pain and loneliness, I can come close to others and strengthen them through my love.

---

[5] Keene, Sam, "Intimacy," *Family Weekly*, January 2, 1984, p. 2.

That's Enough

I can't remove your loneliness or heal your broken heart;
Can't take away the shadows that make your night so dark,
But I can stay beside you when life is getting tough.
If we come close together, that's enough.

I don't have all the answers, and I don't know what to say.
I can't bring you the sunshine or take the rain away,
But I can always hold you when the storm is getting rough.
If we come close together, that's enough.

I had to learn so many things and fail so many times
Before the day I finally realized
If we could take the sorrow from every loss that comes along,
We'd have to take the loving out of life.

I can't remove the dangers from a world so full of fears.
I can't make living safer or take away your tears,
But I can always love you, with a love that you can trust,
And if we can come close together, that's enough.[6]

---

6 Edwards, Deanna, "That's Enough," from the music album *Listen With Your Heart*, Rock Canyon Music Publishers, 777 East Walnut Ave., Provo, Utah, 84604, 1985.

CHAPTER NINE

How Can We Create with Grief?

I stood quietly and reverently before the walls of stone and hedge. Beyond the iron gate, the gentle landscape drew my eyes upward toward the three-hundred-year-old fortress of a farmhouse, Les Barons, the home of Martin Gray. The air was heavy with the sweet smell of mimosa and pine, and the hot July sun was scorching patterns of brown over the green slopes surrounding the estate. The buildings were made of carefully layered fieldstone, and some of the walls were blanketed in thick climbing vines. Carefully trimmed bushes and fruit trees decorated the wide expanse of grass. I stood, paying silent homage to a place that previously had existed for me only in books and pictures. I had come to Europe to tour with my son Shon, and wanted to see Les Barons. So here we were—all the way from the rugged mountains of northern Utah to the wild beauty of Tanneron, a tiny village high above the Mediterranean in the south of France. Only yesterday our train had been moving along the sparkling coastline, past Marseille and Toulon. Just above Cannes nestled the town of Mandelieu, a thriving community on the edge of the sea. The buildings were quaint and colorful, and many of the homes were crowned with rust and ivory tiles. Tropical flowers and palms blended with colorful clothes tied to lines, flying from balconies and windows. Rugged mountainsides were covered with mimosas, fernlike trees that grew thickly on the slopes.

The pilgrimage from our hotel in Mandelieu up the winding mountain road to Les Barons was the most vital part of the journey to Europe. A taxi driver dropped us at the gate and left us there. I had not come to intrude. Privacy and peace were as essential to the people who lived there as water to a thirsty landscape. I had come to listen to the hum of cicadas and birds, singing in concert with the wind that blew up from the sea. I had come to touch the delicate fern leaves of the mimosas and to see the scarred face of the land, blackened tree stumps half buried in the gentle growth of new life. Martin had called it "the martyred earth." I had come because the origins of my own faith were rooted in persecution, and I knew that a desert could blossom as a rose and that man could rise from the ashes of prejudice and pain to live and love again. I wanted to feel the sea breeze on my face and the hot pavement beneath my feet. I intended to walk the six-mile journey back to Mandelieu. It was a sign of respect. My own people had crossed a continent.

A sudden movement inside the gate startled me. I had not noticed the tall man who worked so effortlessly on an old car, hidden by the hedge. His skin was bronze, his hair silver. He smiled quickly. "No, I am not Martin Gray," he said, reading my thoughts. "I am his friend Sidney Shelley. Martin is in Canada on business and will not return for another week. Where have you come from?"

I explained that we had come from the United States and that I was doing research on the life of Martin Gray for a book I was writing about grieving. I had been deeply moved and inspired by his book *For Those I Loved*, a book which was a monument to the power of creative grief. I wanted to learn more, to come to a deeper understanding of how one person can experience so much suffering and live on to create something so beautiful as Martin had done. "I, too, came from the United States," he said, "but most of my life has been spent here in the south of France. Are you on foot?"

"Yes," I replied. "I want to see and feel the land before I return home."

"Then you must come in for some refreshment," he said, opening the gate. "I am sorry I haven't more food in the cottage or I would invite you to lunch. I do have water and fresh fruit, and if you are going to walk back to Mandelieu, you will need something."

We walked into the cool semi-darkness of the little cottage. "Martin built this for his children, in the event they should decide to live on the grounds after they are grown," he explained. "I am only staying for a time. I am a writer as well and am working here on some projects."

Sidney spoke in glowing terms of a long and rich friend-ship with Martin. "He is a man of greatness, but he likes the simple life. He loves to be here, working on the land near his children."

As we were leaving the cottage, a slender little boy suddenly emerged through a small stone gate at the top of the hill and came running down the grass toward us, his golden hair catching the summer light. It was Jonathan, the eight-year-old son of Martin Gray. Instant tears obscured my vision only for a moment. Jonathan was wearing a shirt made of rainbow colors: pink, yellow, green, and lavender. He wore flowing pants of pale lime green, and he had a smattering of freckles above an upturned nose. He welcomed us in flawless English and pressed us to answer a most important question: "What kind of toys do little boys play with in America?"

"My little boy likes toys called 'transformers,' Jonathan," I responded. "I'll send you one when I return home." Then he was off again on a merry errand.

Had Martin Gray himself appeared, I would have been rendered utterly speechless. I was overcome with emotion at the very thought! It was enough to see the shining evidence

of Martin Gray in the smile of his little son. His smile alone
had been worth my trip to France.

Thanking Sidney for his kindness, we excused ourselves
and began the long journey down the mountain. My son,
Shon, and I walked slowly down the winding roads of
Tanneron, a new vista around every bend. It was a narrow,
two-lane highway, with occasional signs of warning
concerning the forest fires that can so quickly sweep the
mountains and consume the vegetation. Here and there,
spouting from the rocks, were the charred remains of tree
trunks. Amazingly, some of the trees were only half burned,
standing in silent testimony to nature's destruction, and the
other halves bearing witness to an amazing ability to bear
fruit and bloom again. Martin had said, "A man can always
plant beside a dead tree a tree of life. As long as man is alive
he can rebuild, even with ruins."[1] As we examined the
evidence of nature's fury, we noticed also that new leaves
and growth were beginning to mask the horrors of fire and
wind. On we walked, focusing on each new scene as it
appeared before us. Stretching below us we could see the
hazy outline of distant mountains and the blue waters of the
Mediterranean, shimmering in the summer heat.

Suddenly I saw it, some yards down the mountain, the
rusty, burned-out shell of a car. It was undisturbed, partially
hidden by new bushes growing up around it. There had
been no pathway made through the thick brush and charred
timber down the steep incline. It was as it had been on
October 3, 1970. Sensing the impact of that sight upon my
heart, Shon held me close.

I thought of the words of David Douglas Duncan when
he wrote a book called *The Fragile Miracle of Martin Gray*.
He said, "There are no scales for weighing sadness, no
vessels for measuring fallen tears. When facing other's
sorrows, one rarely soothes the agony and almost never finds

---

[1] Martin Gray, *A Book of Life to Find Happiness, Courage, and Hope.*

a road to the heart. Understatement or exaggeration often result from searching for words to ease the grief of a friend. That also was a hazard in now telling this story of a man who is worth remembering."[2]

Martin Gray was born in 1925 and lived with his family on Senatorska Street in Warsaw, Poland. He was fourteen years old when Poland was attacked by Hitler's invading armies during World War II. The childhood that should have been his vanished in the carnage of destruction that followed. In the midst of the holocaust, Martin mastered the techniques of survival and escape. He learned to smuggle sacks of wheat to abandoned children in the ghetto, and in the process, kept his own family alive. As a child, he fought against the Nazi invaders of Warsaw. Martin's mother, his two little brothers, and all their friends and neighbors were ultimately discovered in their hiding places and taken to the Treblinka concentration camp. His mother and brothers died there in the gas chambers. While he was in the camp, he lived with the horrors of constant death. He was forced to carry the bodies of his own beloved people to graves of yellow sand. Eventually, he escaped the lower camp by tying himself under a German truck with belts he had taken from dead prisoners. Later, he escaped the upper camp by hiding in a trainload of Jewish clothing.

He tried to warn his people still living in neighboring villages of their impending doom and pleaded with them to fight, but no one would believe the horrors of which he spoke. He eventually made his way back to Warsaw where he and his father led an armed uprising against the Nazis, smuggling arms under the sewers of the city. His father, a fearless advocate for freedom, died in the streets of a sniper's bullet. Martin left the fires of burned-out ghettos and joined the Polish partisans in the forests. In time, he joined the

---

[2] Duncan, David Douglas, *The Fragile Miracle of Martin Gray*, (New York: Abbeville Press Inc., 1979).

Russian army and became a decorated officer, participating in the capture of Berlin on his nineteenth birthday. Disenchanted with the Soviet military, he crossed into American lines where he worked in the counter-espionage efforts.

By then, Martin had only two living relatives: an uncle and a grandmother who were living in New York. Life! Connection! He knew that he must find his grandmother, so he joined the multitudes of stricken European Jews on their way to a fatherland. Theirs was a single hope. America. "You must find my grandmother," he told an American officer. "I'm the sole survivor." Because of the kindness and intervention of that officer, Martin's grandmother was located, and he was able to board a crowded Liberty ship to take him to New York and into the waiting arms of someone who loved him. His reunion with his grandmother was electrifying and unforgettable. He later wrote, "Erect, her nervous white hands clutching her purse, she was at the end of the corridor. I stopped in front of her and she clasped me, imprisoned me in her arms. She was trembling, weeping. . . . She held my face and stroked my cheeks. I was speechless: one word would have opened a yawning gap. The walls would have collapsed, and I would have cried, sobbed with joy and despair, and I would have huddled against her, calling her Mother, asking her to clasp me still more tightly, to hide me in her arms. For so many years, I'd restrained that torrent of fear and sorrow, the need for those soft maternal hands. . . . But I kept silent, stifling my emotions. She was so frail; straining towards me, she would have been drowned in my anguish, shattered by my unhappiness, my memories. It was I who had to protect her, bring her some of my life. She was there, still alive! What more could I ask of her? I pulled her to me, enfolding her in my arms. 'Mamma! Mamma!' "[3]

---

3 Gray, Martin, *For Those I Loved*, (Boston: Little Brown, and Company, 1972), p. 275.

Martin became a U.S. citizen, and recognizing the opportunities for achievement in America, he made a fortune in real estate and imported antiques within ten years of his arrival. He found enormous financial success but still felt deep emptiness in his life. Then his grandmother died. Desolate, he realized he had spent his entire life saying good-bye to those he loved. He knew that it was time to forge ahead, to find a companion, to have children, to build a fortress that would stand as a witness, survive and continue on into a certain future. Sick from too much sorrow and loneliness, he found little to console him. Then he met Dina! And he came face to face with life! He felt as if he had always known her. Time no longer mattered. She was from Holland, blond and radiantly beautiful, with an equally beautiful heart. At the age of thirty-five he had found his happiness! He retired from contracts and business partnerships. Dina despised luxury, and both dreamed of the sea and sun. One day, while exploring the coast and the rocky hills of southern France, they came upon Les Barons. "We're home!" exulted Dina.

It was only a few minutes drive from the sea, and the view was breathtaking. The farmhouse was isolated, crumbling. But it was their fortress. So, there in their hill town on the French Riviera, amidst the strawberry farmers and mimosa cultivators, they rebuilt, redesigned, and created a refuge of peace and serenity. Children came. Martin delivered three of them himself because he wanted to feel their lives in those first moments of existence. Nicole was born first, then Suzanne, Charles, and baby Richard. Blond and beautiful, bursting with life, the children lived on fresh fruits and vegetables. They went barefoot in the sunshine, splashed in the sea, and played among the fruit trees of Les Barons. They were "life" and "home." They were the future!

Then on Saturday, October 3, 1970, the mistral began to blow, a dry wind that ripped through orchards and flattened the yellow grass. It hadn't rained at Tanneron for months, and the peasants were beginning to complain. In the midst of lunch and pleasant conversation, there came through the open window the smell of burning wood. The hill behind their home was ablaze with fire, fire that swept through the dry mimosas and pines at a merciless speed. Martin's children were frightened, and Dina tried to comfort them. Martin remembered the oil supply, a gasoline tank which could explode, only a few yards from the house. He also remembered a bedridden neighbor and felt compelled to help him. "I'll run with the children," Dina shouted.

"Meet me in Mandelieu!" called Martin.

Dina, driving down the winding mountain road with the children and their giant guard dog in the car, was blinded by smoke. In her attempt to turn the car around so she could return to Les Barons, the car slipped down into a ravine. She and the children died while attempting to outrun the flames. With only their bodies, Dina and that heroic dog attempted to shield the children during the final, frantic moments of their lives.

Les Barons, their home, was miraculously untouched by the fire. Both Martin and Dina had been aware of the local peasants' code of never leaving the protection of an old stone farmhouse during a forest fire, but time seemed to be on their side and the children had been frightened. Once again, Martin was the sole survivor. He had been the constant protector of others, yet all his life he had been unable to protect those he loved most: his mother and small brothers, his heroic father, his friends, his people, and now his beloved wife and children. Martin was almost swallowed up in the depths of his own despair and anguish. He waited for the shouts of love and life that he could not hear. Attempts to comfort him failed.

Then a friend responded to Martin's pain, an internationally known photographer named David Douglas Duncan. He lived in Castellaras, France, not far from Tanneron. He and his wife, Sheila, had long since befriended the Grays.

David found Martin at Les Barons wearing an old shepherd's cape to protect the shoulder he had burned while trying to rescue his neighbor. Pictures were taken and sent to the *Paris Match* magazine. Martin was asked to write a book detailing the incredible story of his life. The book *For Those I Loved* became an international best-seller. In almost every country in the world, countless hearts were touched deeply and lives were changed. Martin donated all royalties from his book to a fund promoting fire prevention and to a children's tree-planting program in France. He started the Dina Gray Foundation, an organization dedicated to the preservation of human life. He later remarried and moved back into Les Barons to begin life again. He is now the father of two beautiful daughters, Barbara and Larissa, and a son, Jonathan. His message and his life are captured in a profound statement that has far-reaching implications for us all.

A man must create the world
of which he is the center.
This can be a masterwork:
The painting of an artist,
The piece of a cabinetmaker,
The field of a peasant,
The symphony of a composer,
The page of a writer.
It can be a family.
And when tragedy comes,
as it will, we must take this
suffering into our hands
and, through willpower,
transform it into a fruit
that will nourish us
as we begin life again.
This is the fragile miracle
Hidden within us all![4]

---

4 Duncan, *The Fragile Miracle of Martin Gray*,

After reading the book I grieved for days—not only for Martin's people, but for my own pioneer ancestors who had experienced so much suffering. I grieved for all persons who suffer persecution because of blind prejudice and hatred. I did not want the book, which is by now out of print, to be relegated to the dusty back rooms of used bookstores. I wanted to tell the story again, to share what I had learned: that man can survive pain and suffering and go on to create beautiful things. In order to better understand that "fragile miracle," I made my "pilgrimage" to France, and before leaving that scenic part of the world I had the opportunity to meet David Douglas Duncan, who drove down the winding mountain roads from Casteralles to bring me an autographed copy of his book, *The Fragile Miracle of Martin Gray.* In it he had written, "For Deanna Edwards—wishing you everyday-discovered miracles in life's everyday rainbows. David Douglas Duncan, for Martin, 23 July 1988, Cannes, France."

Before leaving France, I shared a song with David that I had written for Martin Gray.

For Those I Loved!

My eyes have seen the yellow sand,
My ears have heard their cries.
And I have watched a million hands
Reach out to wave good-bye.
I've said good-bye so many times.
I've walked the earth alone,
And I have lived a million lives
Just searching for my home.

I'll climb the highest mountain peaks,
I'll ford the deepest streams.
I'll touch you with my memories
And hold you with my dreams.
For love's the greatest miracle
Our eyes will ever see.
I'm still alive! I will survive!
And you'll live on through me.

I'll build a fortress by the sea
Where earth can touch the sky!
Where sunlight dances on the leaves
And dreams can never die.
Where peace becomes a promise
And truth man's greatest cause.
I'll stand today, I'll show the way,
And live for those I loved!

It has been said that every gain is a loss and every loss is a gain. Roses unfold in such delicate beauty and smell so fragrant, and yet they have thorns. It is amazing that something so beautiful could hurt us. Every wonderful experience, everything in life that is worth reaching out for, can hurt us too.

My friend was talking one day with an older couple. The wife said in animated tones, "My husband and I have been married for forty-seven years and we've never had one argument!"

My friend almost replied with amusement, "Then one of you has been dead for forty-seven years!"

Marriage, having children, all those worthwhile experiences sometimes have painful side effects. But if roses have thorns we must also realize that thorns have roses. For every painful and traumatic experience a rose appears, an undefinable something that deepens and expands the soul and enlarges our vision. We can see more and feel more. I have witnessed, many times, that a person who has known extreme deprivation, one who has lost everything, develops such a deep sensitivity that even the most infinitesimal of delights do not go unnoticed. They no longer take for granted the sound of a child's laughter or the smile on the face of a friend. Pain and deprivation can sharpen our awareness and deepen our appreciation for the smallest of pleasures.

Finding meaning in suffering often leads us into a painful but enlightening journey into the human heart. Grief creates a tremendous amount of energy. This energy, if left unharnessed, can wreak havoc with the mind and body or open the floodgates to a richer experience in living. The source of that energy is love. The creative activity that comes from those who are grieving is love concentrated, love personified, the honest expression of the longing for loving relationships to continue. This creativity need not serve any other purpose than as therapy and the cleansing that occurs from finding expression for deep feelings. But many times it reaches out to others as well. I am incessantly astonished and inspired by the colors and patterns interwoven in the tapestry we call "creative grief."

I received a special note from Janet Rogers:

Dear Sister Deanna,

My father's death was my first experience with losing someone close. I had served in Relief Society presidencies but had never known how to give comfort. When Daddy died, words didn't comfort me nearly as much as the arms that went around me and shared silent tears. Henry David Thoreau said, "All change is a miracle to contemplate." I know from experience that grief brings change, and this kind of change can bring miracles in our understanding.

Grief changes us. Our creative response to that change is the fragile miracle, hidden within us all. "Creative grief" is nothing more than the power of loneliness and the power of love coming together to make something beautiful! Creative grief serves a far greater purpose than mere self-fulfillment. He who can see something beyond his own loss may inadvertently find a cause greater than himself—greater than the pain. It is the act of forgetting self for the sake of others, even for the sake of the one lost, that can result in a richer quality of living and loving—sometimes in ways we least expect. For Christ, the gift of Eternal Life he was giving to us all was greater than the pain of the crucifixion. He never lost sight of the vision—the purpose shining above his own suffering!

Creative grief and recovery involve taking the pain and making something of positive, lasting value with it. It doesn't need to be something monumental. A display in your home, a journal entry, or a new flower garden can be meaningful. If your creativity accomplishes nothing more than an outlet for you and a better understanding about life, it has served its purpose. This process provides therapy for the person who is grieving. It also increases awareness of and respect for others who have the courage to open their hearts and minds in order to learn from their own pain.

Grief means something good only if it changes us for the better and strengthens us. The added dimension of creative grief is that as we use it to clarify and define our feelings, we gain an increased awareness of others. *The unbearable becomes more bearable when it is shared.*

It is that refiner's fire that challenges us to call upon the divine within ourselves and to invite the comfort and presence of the Holy Spirit when we need it most. *Creativity is the essence of life and the evidence of immortality!* As we suffer, creativity can turn tragedy to triumph. We can testify of the ultimate nobility of the human spirit. The pain becomes a tool to create something better in our lives rather than a weapon to hurt or punish us. What we create can be shared with others long after we have passed from man's frail mortal environment. The beauty of this principle is that we can also take our creative capacity with us into the eternal worlds. The phrase, "You can't take it with you," does not apply to creative grief. When we create with loss we are simply practicing with the same potential that we will use in the eternal worlds! We can take with us all we have learned of suffering and all of the sensitivity that accompanied that suffering. We will be better enabled to create in an eternal perspective if we have used our creative energies well in this life.

Pain and love can bring forth such eloquence representative of the finest that is in us. My files are literally filled with poems, stories, and songs that were created by people who were grieving. Each person's creative effort is sacred to me. We find new life in creative thought! It can enrich us and make the old seem new. *All truth that is old is new for the person who discovers it the first time within himself.* The exploration into our feelings, and our attempts to recreate those feelings in music, literature, poetry, letters, or journals, helps us to identify and define what we already know! My husband, Cliff, also a writer, said, *"We don't know what we know until we write it down.* We think in pictures and we need to translate those pictures into verbal symbols. Writing is learning!" Creative effort can awaken and challenge the sleeping giant within us. It can introduce us to ourselves.

I had a teacher, Professor Meyers, who said, "How wonderful to see, to feel, to discriminate purposefully among a thousand remembered perceptions and emotions, and then to put the selected ones into language or action that is as nearly as possible their equivalent; that is life purified and reprojected from the human imagination. Every human being's experiences are actually unique, and are, like his face or fingerprint, exclusively his."

Kahil Gibran said that the great teacher will lead us into the sunlight of our own awareness. Creative grief can become that great teacher. Pain teaches us that we are not strangers after all. We are bonded together in our humanness by our sorrows as well as our joys. When we create with grief we are left with the feeling that we have been in the presence of Someone greater than ourselves, a presence that can lift us into spiritual maturity.

In an article titled "The Creative Journey," from *Banners and Such*, Sister Adelaide said:

Being creative is being yourself, discovering the sources of your own uniqueness. Probing, sometimes with laughter, sometimes with tears, what makes you—you. Building on your own thoughts, ideas and dreams. . . . Freeing yourself from the familiar to launch out into untried ways.

To risk . . . creative activity is an adventure. It may put you in a precarious position, but the growing edge is always into the unknown.

To struggle . . . sometimes you have to wrestle with words

or ideas . . . breaking them open in order to find out what they really mean. The struggle is the process of pulling all the parts together into wholeness.

Over the long haul . . . creativity calls for sustained effort if newness is to grow. The seedling, pushing its way up through hard soil, is in slow, delicate process. With the right environment, it will grow and blossom into something beautiful which can be shared.

When our friends, Vern and Chris Utley, experienced the accidental death of their son, Ben, my brother-in-law, Ted Gibbons, wrote a poem which was greatly appreciated by Ben's family. It captured something of their son's life in a few short lines.

These past days my eyes close always
Into visions of blond hair and joy
Now I know.
His life was a parade of passages,
None too small or too tall
Or too difficult.
He searched them all and owned them,
Clenching at the hours like
Divided oranges.
Demanding the experience
Of every sweet drop—
Savoring and rejoicing
And growing.
He was Monarch of all—
Moments and minutes.
As well ask Caesar
To surrender the world
As to ask him to surrender
An instant of excitement.
Life was not to be lived
But to be loved,
Not to be endured but to be
Embraced.
He could not stand on the

Sidewalk of shadows
And regard the pageantry!
Glory Hallelujah;
He was the star!
Come on! Bring a friend,
Bring all your friends;
Bring laughter and love and light!
He did.
The trembling testimonies
Of lost and silent tears
Of lost and lonely friends.
(Laughing and looking for
Answers to the aching.)
Paint his portrait
In all the brightest colors of
Joy!
No somber grays.
No navy blues. No gloomy blacks.
His life was spring
In new greens and daisy yellow
And rose red.
And the summer of mountains.
Every brush-stroke
Bold and daring!
He was not careful, like
An aged, hollow, husk sliding
Silently into long-awaited
Oblivion.
He flew gloriously
Into the waiting arms
Of eternity.
I remember,
And my eyes close
Into visions of
Blond hair and joy!

When Elder Todd Wilson was killed in Bolivia, Della
Estrada wrote a moving song which was sung at the funeral

service. She dedicated it "to the Wilson Family with love" and titled it "Bless Our Todd Tonight."

> One day a baby learning how to crawl, then walk,
> Then growing up and learning how to sing and talk;
> Then soon a man and going out into the world
> To dedicate himself to God and spread the word.
>
> He was a gentle man, so true and faithful to the cause,
> Of honesty and dedication to his call.
> A friend in need, all they would have to do is call,
> And he would be right there to help them one and all.
>
> He died for us, for the things that we believe,
> He loved us so and wouldn't want us all to grieve.
> He was a martyr for the cause of truth and right.
> When we kneel down to pray, Lord, bless our Todd tonight.
>
> He'll carry on in his life in heaven above,
> He'll see the ones who've gone before and give them love.
> And some sweet day
> When we have proven ourselves worthy,
> We'll be with him again throughout eternity.

When Greg and Carol Ann Gibson lost their little son, Paul, they both wrote verses which were used at the funeral service:

> No one is friendless or Godless
> When he has the companionship of nature.
> Frogs, flowers, people, fish,
> Snakes, butterflies, birds,
> Paul was compatible with all creatures;
> That's why we loved him,
> Why we'll miss him
> And maybe why God wanted him back.
> He knew he was loved, and he "passed it around."
> He liked to be talked to, listened to,
> And tucked in at night.
> Please do this for me, Lord,
> Until I'm so fortunate again.
> His Mom.

Spring entered our hearts with the coming of Paul,
With his love of life, animals, creatures, flowers and all.
He branded our hearts with his love and his smile,
Even though he was here just a little while.
"The Lord giveth and the Lord taketh away,"
But we'll cherish his memory until our last day.
When the day needed brightening, he was usually the one,
The little boy, Paul, who is our son.
Lovable, good natured, everyone his friend,
But winter has set in "'til we meet again."
His Dad.

Jana Miller wrote the following poem after the death of her friend, Mary Obrist:

Thanks to you,
the finer things in life I've learned to appreciate
Like Depression glass, old oak furniture and fancy lace;
Like a small child dressed like Raggedy Ann on Halloween;
Like heart-shaped Valentine cookies
that taste as good as cream;
Like Christmas trees decked from top to bottom with hearts
and angels and all kinds of Santas;
Like holiday gingerbread boys and girls
And grosgrain ribbon that ties a little girl's curls.
Thanks to you, I've learned to be kind,
To be courageous in the face of whatever we find,
To believe in prayer and God's good ways,
To be a friend through all our days.

Our finest creative efforts are only made possible by realizing the greatest depths of our love. Deprivation causes us to reach out into the darkness and capture a star! Martin Gray said, "To achieve inner peace, which alone endures; to make the life of man less cruel; to hold out the hand, the voice, to look to those who call out; you must give yourself projects that enlarge you—that bring your highest energies into play—that oblige you to chose the peak rather than the ditch. Generous projects that make your life generous—and that give free play to the life of man by which it ennobles itself."[5]

We know that some of the world's greatest masterpieces in art, literature, and music were created by grieving people. But some of the great humanitarian organizations have also been started by grieving people. These are the "generous projects" that Martin talked about.

After actor Paul Newman lost his son Scott to an accidental drug overdose, he founded the Scott Newman Foundation which produces audio-visual resource materials to help young people become more aware of the dangers of drug abuse, information that will help them say "No" even in the presence of strong peer pressure.

Darrell Corwin's wife, Cholly, suffered severe brain injuries in an automobile accident in their hometown in Lee's Summit, Missouri. Weeks turned into months while Cholly slept her life away in a long-term care facility. During several visits to Missouri to sing for her, I grew to admire her husband's great strength and courage. He formed an organization called "The Cholly Corwin Fund for Injured Athletes," hoping to find a way to help young athletes who have suffered severe injuries.

The Adam Walsh Center was founded by Reve and John Walsh. In 1981, their six-year-old son, Adam, was abducted from a department store in Florida. During the agonizing searching they learned of the incredible problems of recovering missing children. Beyond their own local police department, they found no other agencies were looking for their son. It was later discovered that he had been brutally murdered. Their resolve to help other parents with missing children led to founding their center, which has issued a call to action at the state and national levels for passage of stronger laws to protect children. The recovery of many

---

[5] Gray, *A Book of Life to Find Happiness, Courage, and Hope*, p. 191.

missing children can be attributed to the awareness of the
public from seeing the pictures on milk cartons, grocery
bags, and T.V. shows. Though their own son died, an
amazing number of children have been safely reunited with
their families because an act of creative grief led to helping
others. John Walsh went further into the cause by hosting a
prime-time television program—"America's Most Wanted."
Many criminals have been brought to justice because of his
efforts.

Candy Lightner, whose daughter died in a drunk driving
accident, founded the group MADD—Mothers Against
Drunk Drivers. Her efforts have helped make our highways
safer and laws tougher against those who drink and drive.
She has since turned over the reins of leadership of her
group to others. "I want to focus less now on how my
daughter died, and more on how she lived."

Orville Kelly, after being given a diagnosis of terminal
cancer, saw a void in communication skills between terminally ill patients, their families and friends. He also saw a
need in the helping professions for open, honest interaction
between staff and patients. His group, Make Today Count,
quickly spread into a national organization which still operates, years after his death.

How do we learn to create with pain? If we are one day
going to create great things when great pain occurs, we must
first begin to create small things with the small hurts in our
lives. Practice this art, for indeed, it is an art. For every
problem and every disappointment we can create something
beautiful. For example, I was on my way to conduct a
conference in California and had to go through the San
Francisco airport. Because of over-booking, several people
were to board the flight going to my connecting city. I was
one of them. It would be a seven-hour wait before another
flight. In those early moments of anger and frustration I had
a decision to make. I could complain loudly to the ticket
agent and wander aimlessly through the airport, or I could

use those seven hours to write letters to some loved ones who had not heard from me in a long time. I chose not to make myself angry and began to write. One letter was written for my friends, the Crawfords, whose son, Paul, had recently been killed in an auto accident. I wrote as though I were speaking to their son:

Paul,

As the sun floods the sky into morning I stir from the very real but suddenly growing distance of my dreams. I saw you there, arms outstretched, your lips parted, about to speak! I wanted to stay with you, to hold you safely in my arms again.

But morning sun pulls you further and further from my reach. Now sleep is heaven and waking is anguish. And I wonder how it would feel to wake and be happy again in your presence. Oh, the peace your touch would bring! Did I take for granted the easy, pleasant awareness of our togetherness? Did I believe the warrior of death would never find our door, never touch the sanctity of our mutual commitment to life? How quickly he slashed through our hopes of growing together and our plan of ever-present reality.

What were you about to say to me as the warm dream became the cold reality? "Come back to life," you seemed to say. "Call upon the best that is in you, for love transcends all loss. Create something beautiful and give it, in my name, to God. Give yourself away, for no loss can take yourself from you. Death cannot diminish our life nor tarnish your brilliant faith, for joy is not the absence of pain. It is the presence of God. Look to this moment and to this day, for this is where life begins!

Know that you will never be alone, for I will be with you. Soon waking will be joy again and sleeping only welcome rest from your weariness. Look for me in all of life, for I will be there in the sunlight that floods your window, the rainbows that struggle through your clouds and the stars that brighten your darkest nights. From your suffering will come the greatest gift, a golden legacy, a bridge to cross for all who will follow after you. I send you all my love, until we meet again.

(Dedicated to Paul Crawford, August, 1985)

The spirit that came over me as I wrote was one of peace and inspiration. Whenever I look back at those long hours in the San Francisco airport I remember the people who benefitted from a note that said, "I love you," and that experience blessed my life too.

Helen Low wrote me a note that said, "There is a train of thought on which each of us must travel when we are alone. The dignity and nobility of our lives, and even our happiness, depends upon the scenery through which that train travels, the baggage which it carries, and the direction that train is traveling."

When we choose to create with pain I am amazed at how the scenery changes, how we leave the unwanted baggage of anger and frustration behind, and travel in the appropriate direction. Creative grief can inspire us to organize a scripture study plan, bake some loaves of bread, write a song, plant a flower, do genealogy work, write in a journal, or do volunteer work. In time, our creative efforts will become an automatic response to losses, both large and small. Instead of asking, "Why did this terrible thing happen to me?" our question will be, "What can I create with this?" The beautiful things we create will help to balance out the pain of loss and help us to grow in ways we never dreamed possible.

It is important to remember, as we travel on the train of life, that we do not have to leave a loved one who dies behind. When special holidays and anniversaries come along, we should not ask, "How am I going to get through this holiday without the one I love to share it?" We should include them first and then plan the holiday in creative ways. If we are going to be together through the eternities we might just as well get used to having them here with us in mortality, if only in spirit. So often, when I have felt special inspiration coming from my father, I say, "Thanks, Dad! I needed that!" Do something special in memory of your loved one, such as taking gifts to the hospital or filling Easter baskets for a needy family.

I was in Germany visiting a family whose daughter had been killed in an accident. They told me of their longing to include her in their thoughts and conversations, and so, during the visit, we talked of Astrid and celebrated her life. While I was there I had a spiritual conversation with her. "Astrid, if I wrote a song for you, what would you have me say?"

The impression came back. "Tell my family to remember me. And tell them, though we cannot speak with words, we can still communicate through the power of love. When they feel love growing inside them, I'll be there."

I quickly took out my pen and wrote a song called "Remember Me."

Remember me whenever you see a sunrise.
Remember me whenever you see a star.
Remember me whenever you see a rainbow
Or woods in autumn colors from afar.

Remember me whenever you see the roses,
Or sea gulls sailing high in a sky of blue.
Remember me whenever you see waves shining in the sun,
And remember, I'll be remembering you.

Remember me whenever you see a teardrop,
Or meadows still wet with the morning dew.
Remember me whenever you feel love growing in your heart,
And remember, I'll be remembering you![6]

An unknown author said, *"What lies behind us and what lies before us are small matters compared to what lies within us!"* Pain helps us to find out what lies within us and to respond with courage, nobility, responsibility, and creativity. It is in that response that we discover our mortal and spiritual potential.

---

[6] Edwards, Deanna, "Remember Me" from the album *Music Brings My Heart Back Home*, Rock Canyon Music Publishers, 777 East Walnut Ave., Provo, Utah, 84064, 1983.

Martin Gray said:

It is important to be faithful to the memory of those we
love. Living shut away in misery is not being faithful. We
must not allow ourselves to be destroyed by the past, but
to remain faithful to it by making it serve as a spring-
board. For life is in progress toward the future. One must
trust in whatever comes. We must continue to plough our
furrow, straight and deep as they would have done themselves, as you would have done with them. For them. To
be faithful to those who have died is to live as they would
have lived, to make them live in us.[7]

When Doris Lund learned that her son, Eric, had
leukemia, she lived the experience with him, supported him,
and encouraged his valiant fight for life. He was a handsome
young man, with a courage and humor that sustained him
through the painful months of his illness. When he was
lying near death in a hospital in New York, he saw the
despair and anguish on his mother's face. He said something
very beautiful and powerful. *"Mom, walk in the world for
me."* What he was really saying to her was this: "Mother, I
don't want my death to diminish your life. I want you to live
better and love better because I was here."

Doris Lund did go on to create the wonderful book *Eric*.
It became a best-seller and eventually a television movie.
When I read the book I was touched by the hope and faith
in Eric's message. If anything we create from our grief
inspires faith and hope in just one heart—even our own—its
purpose has been fulfilled. Eric's words inspired a song that is
used widely in grief counseling, "Walk in the World for Me."

The time has come now for me to say good-bye!
No sad farewells will we share,
For you will live within me, and I will live in you.
No words can say how much we care.

---

7 David Douglas Duncan, *The Fragile Miracle of Martin Gray.*

We walked together on the dusty roads of life,
But kept our eyes upon a star.
We've laughed at the little things and cried along the way.
I've come to know the friend you are!

Walk in the world for me!
Sing a happy melody!
And keep my memory not far away!
May you find that life will bring
All the best of everything!
Take special care of you for me today![8]

---

[8] Op.Cit., *Listen With Your Heart.*

CHAPTER TEN

The Promise

I picked up the faded letter, written to my great-grand-mother Mary Ann Pratt on July 2, 1867, and smiled as I read its conclusion.

I expect to start for the Julesburg terminal, 400 miles west of Omaha, in about six or eight days. I was in hopes to have received a letter from you while here, but I presume you, like myself, did not know of the lengthy tarry that I made here. I am engaged every Sabbath in preaching to the Saints here. I enjoy myself very much, and am blessed with excellent health but still fleshy, not quite bald-headed, beard one foot long, nose crooked, head on one side, phrenological developments not much altered, love of home greatly on the increase! Please give my kind love to our children and be assured of my kind love to yourself. Good-bye until I write again or see you. From yours most affectionately, Orson Pratt.

I learned more about my great-grandfather in that one paragraph than I could have learned in an entire sermon. It gave me a glimpse of his heart. Fascinated by pictures of the man with the long white beard and penetrating eyes, I had gone often to the home of Nels B. Lundwall, an author who took the time to compile many of my great-grandfather's teachings in the book *Masterful Discourses and Writings of Orson Pratt*. We talked for hours in the front room of his little house. Sometimes I had the feeling that Mr. Lundwall knew Orson Pratt personally, because he always spoke of him with knowledge and affection, as if he had been adopted into the Pratt family. He shared personal letters written by Orson as well as research that had helped him in compiling this great work. But the greatest legacy of all was captured in this statement: "On the third day of October, 1879, he died at his home in Salt Lake City. Just before breathing his last, he dictated to President Joseph F. Smith, who took down the words as the dying man uttered them, this epitaph, to be placed upon his tombstone: *'My Body Sleeps For a Moment, But My Testimony Lives and Shall Endure Forever.'*"

I have often felt the impact of that deeply personal statement. Both concepts—pain and promise were there. The body sleeps. The spirit lives. The testimony endures. Bishop Rodney Turner captured the essence of that message when he said:

> Resurrection is the miracle of miracles. It is the universal ordinance by which the Almighty affirms his sovereignty over all creation. It affirms that His agency transcends and comprehends the combined agency bestowed upon mankind. Therefore, His ability to forgive the myriad sins of the human family stemming from its wrongful use of agency far exceeds the sum of those sins. Thus, He has the power to restore all that was lost, to banish all sorrow, wipe away all tears, and to bring the sanctified into His rest where they can partake of His glory. And that is the meaning of the empty tomb.[1]

Any attempt to define faith, especially in the context of grief, requires not only an inward search but a closer examination of those whose faith has been tested to the limits in the refiner's fire of suffering. I believe faith is the most vital tool we have in dealing with loss and separation, and ultimately, the most important concept in religious theology.

---

[1] Turner, Rodney, speech given in a sacrament meeting, 1986. Reprinted by permission.

My effort in the next few pages will be to explore and define that fragile miracle. A scriptural study has led me to conclude that the concept of faith is inexplicably tied to the necessity for hope. Faith leads to hope in Christ. As we cultivate the hope that life is eternal, we move closer to experiencing what faith really is. Those who have a deep, intrinsic faith seem able to call upon that faith for strength and comfort when faced with tragedy.

It is unquestionably difficult for us to define a word or a concept that is subject to many different interpretations. For those who experience sudden and unexplained loss, there seems to be a multitude of conflicting doctrinal messages about faith. Sometimes when we hear others talk about the concept of faith, we get the impression that if we have enough faith we will not die of an accident or catastrophic illness. We can also get the impression that if we live worthily enough we will receive advance spiritual warning of impending danger or potential disaster. If advance warning is predicated upon our worthiness, the grieving person may begin to feel that the accident happened because they were not living worthily enough, and therefore it was "their fault." Many who have lost a loved one through accident or illness may conclude that God answers some prayers for protection but not others, or they may feel they have not been worthy enough to "earn" the blessings of ever-present safety. For many, the simple childhood faith that prompted us to pray when we lost a beloved toy is severely shaken.

Faith does not disappear for those who grieve, but it may be rearranged on the landscape of their lives. When I was a little girl I was given a plastic jar filled with liquid and a miniature scene inside. When I shook it up, tiny snowflakes filled the jar in a minute snowstorm that soon settled back over the landscape. When tragedy comes into our lives, our faith often gets stirred up, even blown about in the emotional turmoil, but eventually it settles back softly to create a new landscape. Often there is a reexamination of the meaning of faith and the role it plays in our lives and even a rearrangement of faith itself. But the new landscape of faith, tested by suffering, can be even deeper and more meaningful than it was before.

Those who grieve tune in much more quickly to the authentic meaning of faith and reject shallow definitions and clichés that don't sound so comforting any more now that the tragedy has happened to them. For some, even the word "blessing" must be redefined. If we are told that a child is taken from us so they will be spared the dangers and pitfalls of life we may begin to feel that a child is being rewarded for dying while we are being punished for living! At the conclusion of many of our church meetings it is not uncommon to hear a petition that we will all be able to return home "safely." On one hand, we are being told how beautiful heaven is, and on the other we are pleading with God not to take us there! People who have lost a loved one may begin to wonder what purpose it serves to pray for the protection of loved ones when we are all still subject to the principle of agency! A person who drinks alcohol and chooses to drive has exercised a freedom of choice that someone else may have to pay a terrible price for!

One night our son, Eric, who was seven years old, knelt to pray. He said, *"Heavenly Father, bless the poor that they will be sort of wealthy. Bless the rich that they won't be so rich. Bless those who aren't too happy that they will be more happy. Bless those who are too happy that they will be sort of in between. In the name of Jesus Christ, Amen."*

I smile now as I think of the strong sense of justice and fairness that prompted Eric's prayer that God would somehow spread happiness out evenly so everyone would get their fair share of it. Yet, he is growing up in a world where unfair things happen and where good people will experience more than their share of pain and tragedy.

In his book *When Bad Things Happen to Good People*, Harold S. Kushner said:

We can't pray that God will make our lives free of problems. That won't happen, and it is good that it doesn't. We can't ask Him to make us and those we love immune to disease, because He won't do that. We can't ask Him to weave a magic spell around us so that bad things will only happen to other people, and never to us. . . . But people who pray for courage, for strength to bear the unbearable, for the grace to remember what they have left instead of what they have lost, very often find their prayers answered. They discover that they have more strength, more courage than they ever knew themselves to have. . . .Their prayers helped them tap the hidden reserves of faith and courage which were not available to them before.[2]

The heroic aspect of faith is to see people call on the fragile miracle within themselves as they walk with pain as a companion. Prayer seems to provide an active kind of energy that helps people cope with loss. When there is nothing else that can be done, we can pray, and prayer can bring physical, as well as spiritual, healing. We pray for many reasons, and one important reason is that we have been commanded to pray. It is right for us to pray for assistance and divine support, to pray over our flocks, our households, and our families. But perhaps it is time to begin to teach our children to pray, not just for fairness all the time, or for constant protection of our loved ones, or that pain will never come into our lives. Perhaps we must learn to pray for the internal strength to cope with loss when it does come, for the capacity to forgive ourselves and others, and for the faith to accept God's love even in the midst of pain and destruction.

Our responding to life's unfairness with sympathy and with righteous indignation, God's compassion and God's anger working through us, may be the surest proof of all

---

[2] Kushner, Harold S., *When Bad Things Happen to Good People*, (New York: Avon Books), p. 125.

of God's reality. The story of Job answers the problem of human suffering, not with theology or psychology, but by choosing to go on living and creating new life. He forgives God for not making a more just universe and decides to take it as it is. He stops looking for justice, for fairness in the world, and looks for love instead. . . . Are you capable of forgiving and accepting in love a world which has disappointed you by not being perfect, a world in which there is so much unfairness and cruelty, disease and crime, earthquake and accident? Can you forgive its imperfections and love it because it is also capable of containing great beauty and goodness, and because it is the only world we have? . . . And if you can do these things, will you be able to recognize that the ability to forgive and the ability to love are the weapons God has given us to enable us to live fully, bravely, and meaningfully in this less-than-perfect world?[3]

In the Lord's Prayer, the phrase "Thy will be done" is still one of the most vital aspects of prayer, not in the sense that all bad things that happen are God's will, but in the sense that we can turn our lives, possessions, and all that we are over to a higher power and have faith in the source of our trust. We can place faith in others when we know they care about us; this is precisely why we can turn all that we are over to God, because He loves us. At that moment of turning our lives over to Him we remember, above all, that He loves us. The deepest longing in the heart of someone who is grieving is the hope that a greater eternal good will emerge from the suffering.

When we sing a hymn together, there is a bearing of collective testimony. The power of that testimony is offered to God as a prayer and is answered with a blessing upon the heads of those who sing it. If collective prayer and the power of faith can help bring peace and equanimity to those who

---

[3] Ibid., pp. 145, 147–148.

are struggling to live and to get well, it can also bring hope and healing to those who are dying. The important thing, in every case, is to store up enough love and strength inside us that we will have that source to call upon when we need it most. Prayer can clean and clear our minds as we lose ourselves in a higher power. It can unclog the junk that accumulates in our minds and allow the sunshine to come through. The more the power of prayer is unleashed in the world, the more good will overcome evil and the greater will be the possibilities of individual peace of mind. Prayer helps us in limitless ways in our mortal condition. It can provide revelation when we need to understand, guidance when we have lost the way, and comfort when we have experienced sorrow and sickness. It is our heart's link with the infinite!

When our neighbors' daughter, Kathy Ball, twenty-five, was told that she was terminally ill with cancer, each person within our local church community was contacted. We were asked to spend the following fast Sunday in a day of special prayer and fasting for Kathy.

Kathy summoned all her family members, and they came to the meeting together. As many of them stood and spoke to us from their hearts, a feeling of peace replaced the disquieting sense of impending loss. I was impressed by the faith that seemed to glow like a candle in the darkness, especially when Kathy herself stood and shared her deep testimony. Upon returning home from the meeting, I called Kathy and asked if she would mind coming to my home to spend an hour or so talking about her concept of faith and how it was that she could meet such a difficult trial with peace and equanimity.

She came to my door looking radiant. Her large, luminous eyes did not register fear or foreboding, and her voice was calm and serene. "You asked about my faith," Kathy said, smiling to herself. "I thought it was interesting because last night Mom and I were talking. She was saying that she admired my courage. I don't have courage, but I have a lot of faith. When you called and said we were going to discuss that I was surprised. But it's not courage, and it's not 'me.' It's the light and knowledge that I receive through the gospel and from my family. I know there is nothing to worry about in death. That holds no fear for me. The scriptures tell us that Christ will take away the sting of death. He has conquered death, and whatever I go to will be better than what I have here. My family will have to grieve, and I feel sorry for that, but I am going to be on the other side, being busy and happy, and I hope they will stay here and be happy."

"That is a very important point you just made, Kathy," I said. "So often when a child in a family dies there is a tremendous emotional upheaval. That's a normal part of grieving, but some families go on grieving for so many years that happiness eludes them. What I hear you saying is that you really want your family members to continue to celebrate life and not be unhappy too long because you are leaving them."

Kathy's eyes sparkled mischievously. "That's what I want them to do—like we are doing this week—just having fun."

"What are you doing?" I asked curiously.

"Well, for example, my sisters and I had to go out shopping; and we went to buy milkshakes. We sat in Hamburger World and told funeral jokes. We were laughing so hard we were almost rolling on the floor! The couple sitting at the next table were appalled. They would have been even more appalled had they known that I was dying. But it helps! Laughter helps us to deal with it!"

"A sense of humor is so important," I affirmed. "One day I received a call from a young woman named Mary. She wanted to come to one of my workshops and asked when the next one would be. She was a bit shy about telling me her full name and finally confessed her name was 'Mary Death,' pronounced as it is spelled. She said it was not an uncommon name in New Zealand where she came from, but it certainly was in the United States. She said that she worked with dying patients for the San Diego Hospice and that her name has been a problem in her work. She does not want to go around wearing a name tag, so whenever patients ask her name she quickly replies, 'Mary Christmas!'"

Kathy laughed. "The importance of humor is sometimes hard to get across to the people I love most. I hate worry! I can't stand it! Worry is not one of my traits. There is no point to it. Concern is constructive but worry is destructive. It does the person who is worrying no good, and it does the person they are worrying about no good."

"Kathy, I don't think I ever stopped to analyze the difference between those two concepts, and it interests me. Could you describe that difference for me a little more?"

"Worry is a raking of the soul, an internal anguish that fights reality and destroys you when you ought to be putting that energy outward and showing your love," Kathy explained. "Concern means if you are concerned about someone you will do everything in your power to help them. In many cases, such as in terminal illness, all you can do is pray, and that is such a tremendous gift for the person who is in pain! Concern is Christlike love, doing everything you possibly can do for someone, especially fasting and praying. In this past week I have been amazed at the strength I have received! I want to be independent and do everything I can for as long as I can. I don't want to be waited on. And what I love is when I call people and tell them I don't have very long to live. The conversation starts out seriously, and then I get across to them that I am fine and we end up laughing. But what I really want to hear people say is, 'We'll be praying and fasting for you.' Whether they are here or far away, that is the most important thing they could be doing for me right now. It gives me the most strength. However, it bothers me when people ask in their prayers for me to get well. That's not what I want them to pray for. I know their intentions are good, but it makes me feel uncomfortable."

"Kathy, I am so glad you came over today," I said, grateful for what I had learned from her. "I guess what I want to convey to you is that you really are my teacher! You are speaking from a point of view that is at the heart of life, and since you are there, on that very brink between heaven and earth, you have a perspective we don't have. You have a great deal to teach us. If we build walls that are too thick, whether those walls are built from worry or fear of death, we are not going to hear you, and it will be hard for you to get your message across!"

"You're right!" Kathy agreed. "I catch myself lecturing people. When I see them smoking or driving recklessly, I want to run over to them and say, 'Hey, look! You may not have much more time to live!' I want to grab their cigarettes and say, 'Do you know what you'll go through when they tell you that you have lung cancer?' But I can't do that. I just lie low. They'll make it. I have to say, 'That's okay. Live your own life!' But if I share all this with you, Deanna, someone who hasn't heard it will pick up your book, and they might be able to find the answers. Maybe they'll spend their time wisely, and they won't have so many arguments with people they love, and they won't ignore health and safety rules. And maybe," she grinned, "they won't worry so much! I may die of cancer, but I will not have an ulcer! And many people don't understand that! My biggest concern is how people will respond to my illness. I have a hard time convincing people that I am fine! I separate myself into two entities. There's a 'me' that is all right. I'm fine, and I will always be as long as I have faith and hope in Christ. And then there's my health. My health is lousy, but that doesn't affect me. That's what I want people to understand!

"People tell me not to give up hope," Kathy summarized. "But I haven't! I'm being realistic! How can I give up hope when my faith is in Christ? Faith does not mean that if you live righteously you're never going to suffer any problems. It means that you'll be able to handle them! It's putting yourself in God's hands. It's saying, 'I'm yours.' It's turning your life over to Him. I'm trying to think of what I told Mom last night about faith. It's just a belief that whatever happens will be the will of God and that it will be in my best interest. I know that my Heavenly Father wants me to have joy! The scriptures tell us, 'Man is that he might have joy,' and I totally believe that! Knowing that my life is in Father's hands, how could I question what will happen? He wants me to be happy. If I follow His will, I will be happy!"

Several important truths were revealed in my conversation with Kathy. One was the difference between worry and concern, dealing with problems as they come rather than worrying about and anticipating problems. She pointed out that a destructive worry pattern was an obstacle to a faith that embraced a Christlike love and concern. Not only did Kathy view it as an obstruction to faith and the spiritual healing process, but it actually became a threat and was consciously avoided.

Another important aspect of our conversation was a better interpretation of "hope," and a greater understanding of the meaning of the phrase, "God's will." Some might interpret that to mean that everything that happens on earth is God's will and that all accidents, diseases, wars, and earthquakes are caused by God for some divine purpose. Kathy's interpretation was that, in spite of accident and illness, God's greatest will for us is joy, strength to cope with our difficulties, inner peace, and eternal exaltation. It is not God's will that we live indefinitely in this mortal state. We all have to die to be resurrected and achieve immortality. So our hope is anchored in Christ—not in whether or not our death is imminent.

Before her death, Kathy sent bouquets of flowers to her friends to comfort them! Whenever I think of Kathy today, I have an image of her shortly before her death. Chemotherapy treatments had caused her hair to fall out and her energy level had been greatly depleted, but she wanted to give a special gift to her mother for Mother's Day. Kneeling in front of her house, wearing a scarf about her head, she was planting pink, purple, and white petunias. They bloomed gloriously that year as they have every year since her death. Russ and Hazel Ball keep the promise they made to Kathy by planting the flowers in memory and celebration of her faith.

Our neighborhood experienced much sadness when, over a period of a few short years, several members of our ward died. One was a handsome young man of seventeen. Robert Talbot was a very accomplished young man, both spiritually and intellectually, and was very dear to our family. Rodney Turner was our bishop at the time of Robert's death, and he shared some profound thoughts at the funeral service that clarified important concepts about the pain and the promise of grief.

One of the concerns expressed immediately after Robert's death was that it seemed to contradict his patriarchal blessing which indicated that he would live and would have a very successful and rewarding life. This is a problem which confronts many people when hopes, plans, dreams, and blessings seem not to be fulfilled. We usually have certain clichés, and I have heard them all in the last few days: "The Lord took him because he was needed on the other side"—"It was God's will"—"His patriarchal blessing will be fulfilled in eternity." All of this may be true. On the other hand, I think sometimes we fail to understand how God interacts with man and the relationship of blessings to the overall design of the plan of salvation. Because of that, in an effort to rationalize these apparent contradictions, we do come up with these typical answers. We must understand that whatever blessing we may receive in this world is subject to the principle of free agency. Free agency operates both positively and negatively. It has a profound affect on the course of our lives. This is a lone and dreary world where the slings and arrows of outrageous fortune are often the rule rather than the exception. It really doesn't matter how long we live. It matters very much how well we live. Had Robert lived to the age of Methuselah he could not have obtained more blessings, or rendered greater service, or received more joy than he will by leaving us at the age of seventeen. Now is the time to trust in the infinite wisdom and mercy of the Lord, because our testimonies must transcend our mortal condition. A testimony must not be based upon good health, wealth, prosperity, popularity, or earthly success. A testimony must stand above the earth and all the clouds and in the clear light of the Eternal Son. We have to measure our love and our commitment to the Lord in terms of the degree to which we cling to it in the dark night of the soul, when He seems to have forsaken us. Then you know, in that dark moment, how much you really love and how much you really believe. Jesus was scourged, spat upon, mocked, and crucified. He took it all upon Himself and submitted patiently to the will of the Father. Will you submit patiently to the will of your Father in the hour of darkness?

Our greatest tests are in adversity, as well as prosperity. Through man's agency, Robert's life has been taken. Through God's agency it will be restored in perfection, in glorious, immortal youth. Brothers and sisters, we are that we might have joy. Happiness is the object and design of our being. All is well!

When faith is crying out for definition, the Spirit often draws itself to what is most helpful to us in time of need. When I have asked people what faith means to them, many of their answers have warmed my heart.

"Faith is the ability to say, 'My glass is half full' while others are saying, 'My glass is half empty.'"

"Faith is the ability to believe; to believe in little kids and loved ones and God and all that is good."

"Faith is belief in a God who has created us and believes in our ability to cope with reality."

"Faith is knowing that no matter what happens, even if it isn't all right, I will be all right."

"Faith is the power to love, the power to pray, the power to create, the power to care, the power to share, and the power to give thanks."

The pioneers who came West visualized a desert in a mountain wilderness, blossoming as a rose. It was a kind of collective vision and unified faith that could not foresee who would live and who would die before the journey's end or what hardships would befall them. It was a vision so powerful that attaining the goal was worth the price they would have to pay to achieve it. What constituted the vision? Religious freedom, a vast land to tame, cities to build, trees to plant, crops to grow, and missions to fulfill. These dreams sustained the pioneers when their most difficult trials came. They were willing to walk with death and pain as constant companions because their spiritual eyes could see the promise of what lay ahead. The gift of vision that inspires such a sense of mission is a goal all of us can attain.

The entire process of grief, the pain and the promise, can all be found in a song of praise that inspired an entire people as they crossed a rugged wilderness. "Come, come, ye Saints, no toil nor labor fear, but with joy wend your way. Though hard to you this journey may appear, grace shall be as your day."[4]

Whenever I sing that song, I can see it all: the journey and the destination, earthly trials, and eternal promises. I see the courage of men, women, and children whose faith in God was immovable, who knew the meaning of grief and were not afraid of its process. This is our heritage, and it can be our legacy. The song ends with the moving words, "All is well." All is well, and will be well, if we can remember Kathy's simple words: "How can I give up hope when my faith is in Christ?"

My husband, Cliff Edwards, expressed that simple faith in a poem titled, "All is Well."

The limbs of trees stand out sharply
Against the starkness of the gray sky.

---

[4] Clayton, William, "Come, Come Ye Saints," *Hymns*, no. 30.

Snow is falling, falling,
Each flake is pure crystalline beauty.
I catch one on the tip of my tongue,
Only a pinprick of cold, ever so small.
Then all is gone.
One tiny burst of essence, then nothingness.
Flakes fall into my palm.
Ever so quickly do they disappear.
How can this be?
Their beauty is so rare,
Their form so delicate,
But so soon they are gone, never to return,
Like the march of humanity across the pages of time.
First here, and then they are no more.
How can this be?
Is there no reason for all this?
I feel the stirring within.
He is there.
War, death, destruction,
The creators of nothingness.
They are not what is.
Can you see it?
The purpose and cause of all!
It sounds loudly in my head
Like a thump, thumping.
I know!
There is rhyme and reason.
I can feel His presence.
I am encompassed round about.
I am carried away.
The snow is falling, falling,
Small puffs of white against my cheek.
The air is chill but unfelt.
I am warmed by the Great Purpose.
The silence gathers.
Only the quiet falling of snow.
Now only the sound of my own footsteps
Against the mounds of softness
Piled up before me.

The darkness gathers.
There is but a single point of light against the black.
I make my way forward.
The rush of cold air.
A worried glance,
A gentle touch,
The fire—warmth—
All is well!

The afternoon sun sent shafts of light into a hazy blue sky. We had just left the emerald green Jordan River and had enjoyed lunch with our tour guide, Dan Rona, and a small group of Church members. At the Sea of Galilee we had a marvelous lunch of various salads, mostly spiced vegetables and sauces, and the big treat, St. Peter's fish! Dan told us that the coin in the mouth of the fish, retrieved at the instruction of Jesus, was probably from this wide-mouthed fish which anciently lived in the lake. We went up the mountain to where Jesus had preached the Sermon on the Mount. Dan pointed out that this is where much of the new law was given. Jesus expanded the spirit of the law, contrary to the Law of Moses, in that sermon. We sat in the shade of palms, enjoying the glimpses we could see of Galilee and we read the Sermon on the Mount from our scriptures. As we read, the awareness came over me that many of the statements in the sermon are promises he made to us personally. *"Blessed are they who mourn, for they shall be comforted."* I wondered, as we read, if perhaps our Savior has a divine network of people operating on the earth whose hearts, hands, and talents are used by Him to keep that promise.

I believe that many who enter the helping professions, those who are "called to care," become, in a special way, the hearts and hands of comfort, a part of that divine network. I was privileged to receive the following letter from my physician, Tom Myers, telling me of his personal experience that moved and inspired me:

Dear Deanna,

A few years ago, in the fall, I made my last house call to a sweet and very dear old lady. Provo had an uncommonly colorful autumn that year, and people were talking excitedly about the drive over Mt. Nebo. From her bedroom window, the late afternoon sun wound brightly through the yellow leaves.

She died while I stood by her bed.

I knew she was dying. In fact, I had my stethoscope on her frail, translucent skin as her heart fumbled itself into a fatal rhythm. In keeping with my training, I reached into my bag for the drug that would save her—one push of the clear liquid into her veins, and the heart would sigh and resume its work. She looked at me with kind eyes and said nothing. It was painless to her.

Around the room was shoulder-to-shoulder family. It was more like a crowded marriage in a sealing room than a death watch. The five children were there—all in some way touching their spouses, holding hands, arms around each other. One couple was doing both. The grandchildren were squeezed in like so many socks in a suitcase—quiet and curious.

The oldest son from "back East" was there. I looked up at him and was met by his icy arrogance. He and I had had words about letting Grandma die at home.

"Listen," he had said to me a few days ago, "I have nothing against you personally. You are probably a well-qualified doctor in your field. But I feel strongly that we need a cardiologist for Mom." The family stood uncomfortably by and deferred to the overbearing wisdom of the older brother.

He went on. "If Mom were with us in New York, we would have long ago had her in the hospital. Probably in the cardiac unit." He shot a look at his sister.

I could feel the defensive anger surge like a firestorm. After all, what other doctor would have made house calls two or three times weekly for this sick old lady—and most of the time for free! And where was this "back-East" brother during all the tough times of the previous year!

The sister shook her head. She had cared for the little grandmother for the past eight years. She and I had had long discussions about death and dying. Her children and I had talked. We had even discussed Grandma's sweet little last givings-away.

"This is from my trousseau," Grandma had said, passing a beautiful handkerchief to a granddaughter. "I did it myself, and I want you to have it. There's a story with it. I want you to have that, too. "

One by one during the past three months, she had given away the last of her personal things. There remained only nightgowns, a picture, and a few toilet articles.

At first it broke the children's hearts. But we talked about death. And goals. They learned to accept the little gifts with tears, hugs, and fond, tender words.

But one thing was clear: Grandma did not want to go back into the hospital. She had made them all promise and had exacted the same promise from me. Once she whispered in my ear, "I'm so glad we found you!"

I looked at the oldest brother with what I hoped was a calm demeanor.

"I can see that you feel strongly about this. Do you have a few minutes to talk about it?" He replied that there was really not much to talk about. A friend of his in Salt Lake City had recommended a certain doctor, and he was going to take Mom to see him on Friday. But he sat down anyway.

We talked for over an hour. I tried to let him see that all was well. I was quick to compliment the family on the long hours of care. We talked, listened, and did not agree. However, he reluctantly gave in a day later. The sister called to let me know.

So, on the day of her death, alone at her bedside, under the watchful eyes of them all, I made a decision to leave the medicine in the bag. I couldn't think of anything to say to her. I looked back at her soft white hair on the clean sheets. She smiled and whispered, "Thank you."

I am certain to this day that she felt my struggle and was aware of my decision.

I stood up. "This would be a good time for each of you to give Grandma a hug," I said.

Some of them began to cry. One by one they bent over the bed. She seemed to be whispering in each ear. She was controlling things. She pushed each one away quickly. I think that she knew that there was very little time. I was surprised that she was still alive.

The hugs were almost done—only about six or seven more. She looked at me. Really she looked through me to the door behind me. She smiled and said, "Just one more minute, Joseph."

Joseph was the name of her husband who died twenty-six years before.

She hugged the last small child, whispered in the tiny ear, and sighed. She was dead.

I called the mortuary and took care of the necessaries. The family seemed not to notice me, and, having done all I could do, I started to leave. A rough hand on my shoulder turned me around. The "back-East" brother looked at me with red eyes. His shoulders were shaking a little as he sobbed. He took my hand and shook it. Finally he said, "Thanks," and he turned back to the family.

I drove home in the twilight and thought that few experiences offer more hope to us than does death.

One of our family traditions is to celebrate Thanksgiving in our cabin in the mountains of Wyoming. This rustic setting is a perfect retreat away from the frantic rush of civilization. On these occasions, Thanksgiving becomes a truly old-fashioned holiday, filled with wonderful fun, when we build snowmen with the boys, eat pumpkin pie, have long talks around a dancing fire, and take long walks through falling snow.

After dinner on one such Thanksgiving, I allowed myself the luxury of a few hours of solitude in the wilderness while other family members were playing games and finishing off calorie-laden leftovers. I shall never forget the pine trees and quaking aspens, edged in white lace, twinkling in the sun. It was a clear day and the mountains looked very comfortable as they cradled their broad shoulders against blue satin skies. It seemed almost irreverent of me to be trudging across the incredible, untouched surface of snow. My boots made a soft sound as I moved up the winding road, but when I stopped I could hear wind whispering in the pines and the echo of distant birds. The sun warmed my cheeks in the crisp wind, and I could see the curious eyes of a porcupine that had waddled into a thicket for safety.

As I crossed the bridge at the foot of the mountain, I noticed the stream had formed a pool, surrounded by snow-drifts piled high on the banks. The water was so crystal clear that it mirrored a perfect reflection of the brilliant sky and the nearby quaking aspen trees. I pushed through the snow to the edge of the pool and stared into the water. I had the strange sensation that I was standing in the sky looking at the trees upside down!

Suddenly, I was face-to-face with *faith*. I did not have to reach out and touch the smooth white bark of the trees to know they were there. They were reflected clearly in the image of the water. I did not have to reach out and touch the hand of God to know that He was there, for I could see His image in the face that peered with such intensity into the pool. I bent down and scrawled four words across the white paper of snow. *"You are a miracle."* I felt intensely that each person on the earth is a miracle.

We are all children of God, the reflection of His presence on the earth. All that I saw around me was the evidence of His creation. And I could communicate with Him and with loved ones on the other side through the power of love, which is perhaps the ultimate proof of all! Since love is the one eternal factor that binds us in mortality and cannot be destroyed, so love can bind us in immortality.

The author of that love is the Savior. His greatest gift to us, the gift of Eternal Life, was literally handed to us through the gateway of grief. So perhaps there truly is something sanctifying and sacred about pain, and no matter how dark that pain becomes, there is always a light at the end of it!

Be My Light

When our hearts have been broken
And dreams are forgotten
It's easy to feel all alone.
But He'll pick up the pieces and put them together
And tell us that we are His own.

When we go through our trials
It seems like there's never been
Someone who's been there before.
But alone in a garden He gave us forever,
He could not have given us more!

There's a light at the end of the tunnel, I know,
For He promised this darkness would end.
Precious Lord, give me strength for the journey ahead!
Be my light! Be my guide! Be my friend![5]

---

[5] Edwards, Deanna, "Be My Light," from the album, *Two Little Shoes*, Rock Canyon Music Publishing, 777 East Walnut Ave., Provo, Utah, 84604, 1980.

MUSIC BY DEANNA EDWARDS

SHARE LOVE'S LIGHT (Cassette and songbook): Share Love's Light, Seasons, Keep Me Next to You, My Mother's Hands, The House I Used to Live In, Love Is Me, Am I Beautiful to You?, Still Like New, Where Did I Come From?, Love Is All That Matters.

MUSIC BRINGS MY HEART BACK HOME (Cassette): Take My Hand, Where Have All the Dreamers Gone?, Teach Me to Die, Peacebird, Music Brings My Heart Back Home, Brand New World, The Littlest Angel, You're Going Home, Remember Me, That's Enough.

REMEMBER ME (Cassette and Stereo LP): Holding Hands with God, Remember Me, The Hearts You Break, I'm Glad That God Chose Me, Since You Came into My Life, I Am Love, Plenty of Time For You, The Littlest Angel, Someday I'll Find You, Love Is Out There Too.

TWO LITTLE SHOES (Cassette and Stereo LP): I Can Give You Love, Two Little Shoes, Be My Light, Loving Is the Only Way, Wanted: One Family, If We Should Say Goodbye, I Can't Believe My Eyes, Find a Friend, I Don't Believe in Heroes, Butterflies.

MUSIC, LAUGHTER, AND TEARS (Cassette, LP, and songbook): Sunrise, Just Around the Corner, My Road, All the Love in the World, Don't Be Afraid, Keep Me Warm, Music, Laughter, and Tears, My Mother's Hands, Play Clothes, Live Each Day.

A SONG IS A GENTLE THING (Cassette): A Song Is a Gentle Thing, Before It's Too Late, Your Favorite Songs, Shanti Nilaya, Who Will Listen?, Why Can't We?, I Lost the One Who Loved Me, You're Only a Memory Away, A Rainbow from You, Walk in the World.

PEACEBIRD (Cassette): He Is Your Brother, Peacebird, I'll Hold You in My Arms When I Get Home, Catch A Little Sunshine, Teach Me to Die, Brand New World, Take My Hand, Folks Don't Kiss Old People Anymore, The Right to Live, Put My Memory in Your Pocket.

WITH A SONG IN MY HEART: DEANNA EDWARDS AND MICHAEL BALLAM: With a Song in My Heart, Some Enchanted Evening, Bali Hai, Sunrise, Sunset, Kiss Her Now, Old Man River, Something Wonderful, O Danny Boy, Guten Abend, Gut Nacht, He Shall Feed His Flock, Believe Me, Somewhere My Love.

A HEALING AFFAIR OF THE HEART (Double CD) *Disc One:* Angel Unaware, Amazing Grace, Holding Hands With God, Shanti Nilaya, Bird With a Broken Wing, I Don't Believe in Heroes, Listen With Your Heart, Where Have All the Dreamers Gone?, Am I Beautiful to You?, My Road, Teach Me To Die, If We Should Say Goodbye, The House I Used to Live In, You Are Like a Color, Walk in the World for Me, Broken Windows. *Disc Two:* Two Little Shoes, Someone Who'll Stay, You're Going Home, Keep Me Next You, The Hearts You Break, Remember Me, Give Yourself Away, Wanted: One Family, Yes—or No—?, I Am Love, That's Enough, Since You Came Into My Life, The Littlest Angel, Today is The First Day.

A HEALING AFFAIR OF THE HEART, (Cassette, Vol. 1): Same as CD, Disc One.

A HEALING AFFAIR OF THE HEART, (Cassette, Vol. 2): Same as CD, Disc Two.

TALK TAPES WITH MUSIC

THE LANGUAGE OF LOVE: WITH MICHAEL BALLAM (Two cassettes): Michael first heard Deanna sing in the Logan High School production of *South Pacific* when she was seventeen. Years later, their paths crossed again as Michael was seeking help for a dying friend. Their musical journeys had taken them in different directions. Michael was led to the great opera stages and concert halls of the world singing for royalty in Europe and performing the classic works of Puccini, Beethoven, and Mozart. Deanna's journey led to quiet hospital rooms and nursing homes throughout the country, where she sang to the sick and suffering, the lonely, and the dying. She used her songwriting skills to become a voice for the hurting. They discovered that their unique differences have aided in lifting them both to renewed understanding of their own musical missions. In these tapes they bring the dynamic combination of these two different worlds together. Michael and Deanna will inspire and delight you as they bring a new song to your heart—a song you will want to sing forever! Includes songs such as: Wanted: One Family, Two Little Shoes, If We Should Say Good-bye, and Be My Light.

SEMINARS WITH MUSIC

LEARNING TO LIVE WITH GRIEF (Two cassettes): Deanna teaches us that grieving and loving are very much the same thing, and that grief can lead to growth. She explains, "We do not need so much protection from pain as we need the boldness to face it. Even when a loved one is lost we do not lose our capacity to love. If we choose to love we must also have the courage to grieve. I have learned that joy is not the absence of pain. It is the presence of God. This means that in whatever circumstance we find ourselves, all of us have access to joy." Both her book and teaching tapes help us cut through all the clichés and give real help for coping with losses of all kinds. Includes songs such as: Walk in the World for Me, Remember Me, and That's Enough.

WHOEVER YOU ARE, I LOVE YOU (One cassette): Best known for her loving spirit, Deanna says, "The Savior's message was love. He devoted his life to teaching us how to love because He knew that if we could learn to do that, we would be able to come back into His presence. To love is to affirm another person's right to be. Every person is like a color of the rainbow and our color will never be duplicated by anyone." In this special seminar you will be lifted, comforted, and inspired. Includes songs such as Love Is Me, and If We Should Say Good-bye.

SHARING THE GIFT OF LOVE (Four cassettes): In these tapes Deanna discusses in detail the reasons why music is a therapy. She will share her ideas about music as the universal language and how to use it in hospitals and nursing homes. She speaks of the five principles of caring that will assist us as we prepare for the most exciting of all adventures; the journey of love into the human heart.

Cassette 1: Society's Attitudes: The Scale of Life
Cassette 2: Music in Therapy: The Universal Language
Cassette 3: Making Memories Live: Music Says What I Feel
Cassette 4: Creative Grief and Recovery: The Five Principles of Caring

Some of the above tapes are distributed by Covenant Communications, Inc., P.O. Box 416, American Fork, Utah 84003-0416.

For more information, call Deanna at (801) 375-1453, or write to her: 777 East Walnut Ave., Provo, Utah 84604.

The author wishes to express her deepest gratitude to the following individuals, whose contributions are used by permission in this book:

Sister Adelaide
Kathy Albrecht
Vern Albrecht
Father Rick Arkfeld
Brent A. Barlow
G. Bradford
Kathy Bradford
Trina Brander
Bonnie Bright
Steven L. Channing
Roger Chapman
Christie Lund Coles
Laurene Cuningham
Carol daSilva
Glen Davidson
Becky Edwards
Cliff Edwards
Della Estrada
Elizabeth Field
Dawn Star Fire
Jean Gardner
Ted Gibbons
Greg and Carol Ann Gibson
James A. Goodman
Wanda Hilton
Marsha Canterbury Jones
Sara King
Annabelle Koran
Sharon Kubie
Shauna Larsen
Ted Lofgreen
Helen Low

Betsy Luce
Margie Mehr
Michael McLean
Jana Miller
Matt Muldoon
Tom Myers
Laurie Nelson
Roy Nichols
Dick Obershaw
Walter "Buzz" O'Connell
Lynette Olsen
Carol Lynn Pearson
Charlotte Quick
Miriam Rich
Isla Paschal Richardson
Ranier Maria Rilke
Janet Rogers
Kay Simmons
Betty Skow
Margaret Snyder
Nadine Starr
Ora Pate Stewart
Charlotte Thomas
Rodney Turner
Carol Turno
Karen Wagner
Elaine Wilson

Notes:

Notes:

Notes:

Notes: